Soil Mates

Companion Planting
for Your Vegetable Garden

By Sara Alway

QUIRK BOOKS
PHILADELPHIA

Library of Congress Cataloging in Publication Number: 2010930252

ISBN: 978-1-59474-445-7

Printed in China
Typeset in Pauline and Bembo
Designed by Jenny Kraemer,
based on the design by Sara Alway, justAjar design
Content editing by Mary Ellen Wilson
Content review by Kelle Carter
Illustrations by Wai
Recipes courtesy Susanna Franklin
Production management by John J. McGurk

Distributed in North America by Chronicle Books
680 Second Street
San Francisco, CA 94107

10 9 8 7 6 5 4 3 2 1

Quirk Books
215 Church Street
Philadelphia, PA 19106
www.irreference.com
www.quirkbooks.com

♥

Table of Contents

Foreword

GARDEN PREPARATION, PLANNING & CARE

Foreword

The way I see it, the ability to grow things is something we're all born with. Give children a watering can, and they'll shower everything in sight. They know that plants need water. I'm not saying that growing something is as easy as watering it, but it's a start.

It seems that in this modern world of ours, people have forgotten how to do a lot of the simplest and most basic things that used to come as second nature. We seem to think that only the most educated in the field of agriculture are able to grow our food. Not true—anyone can have a garden! Start with a small container, and, as your garden grows, so will your imagination and the possibilities, too.

This is my seventh year growing food. I began at the Seeds of Change Research Farm, where I became enamored with the art of nurturing plants. Now my fiancé and I are running our own market garden in Colorado. This book is a great "how to" for the beginning gardener and an easy reference for the avid grower. Companion planting is a relatively effortless way to improve the health of your soil and crops. The plants do all the hard work; we just plant them where they want to be.

Even growing on a large scale, the information in this book is relevant and applicable. It provides all the details to grow food in any capacity, and the recipes supply gardeners with delicious and easy ways to eat their work. Cooking with food you grow is a true delight, and even the novice can create a flavorful meal when using fresh ingredients.

The best way to learn how to grow a garden is just to go outside and grow a garden. Start small, take notes of what worked and what didn't, and keep maps of where crops were planted. Over the years, you'll learn a lot from the information you gather at the end of each season. Gardening is something you can do. Just dig up some time and plant yourself in the backyard.

—Kelle Carter, Farmer, Southern Roots Farm

What Is Companion Planting?

Just like people, plants are searching for the perfect companion. Someone who brings out the best in them, makes them feel comfy, keeps the bad influences away. Just as people search the world over for their soul mate, plants hunt gardenwide for their *soil* mate. And it's our job as gardeners to help these lovelorn veggies find each other.

Gardeners have learned to maintain high-yielding crops without chemicals simply by placing certain plants together in a garden bed. A conscientious placement of plants that are beneficial to each other—known as companion planting—will boost your harvest while reducing your work battling weeds, pests, and diseases. Most important, you won't be reaching for the chemicals because the plants will be doing a lot of the heavy lifting. They'll be attracting good bugs, birds, and animals; hiding the harvests from predators; and creating a more natural biodiversity that is less taxing on the soil.

As the ultimate dating manual for your vegetables, this book will clue you in on simple tips and help you create the perfect symbiotic relationships between your plants. Once nestled in bed together, your veggie companions will thrive, making for a happy and productive garden.

HORTICULTURAL MATCHMAKING

Each pair of soil mates begins with a succinct but fun description of both plants—their general features, their overall needs and desires—in essence, what makes them a **Love Match**. Next, **My Place or Yours** details how best to place your companions to maximize their benefits to each other, complete with a handy planting illustration. Then come the **Plant Profiles**. Think of these as snapshots of the plants that highlight their special little quirks and unique offerings, the bugs that bug them, and their sordid third-party attractions. Noted are their:

Turn-Ons Let's face it: Everyone has a soft spot for special treatment, including plants. Try these tips and tricks to keep your soil mates happy and productive.

Turn-Offs You know the type. They hog the sunlight, drink all the water, and then expect their partner to produce in the garden bed. Try to avoid these situations if you want garden harmony.

Needy Alerts Be warned! These types will always be asking for more fertilizer, more water, more sun, more everything. Though they are needy, if you give them your attention, they will reward you generously. So lavish your love with impunity.

Stalker Alerts Always be on the lookout for those pesky stalkers—of the insect or animal variety.

Love Triangles Sometimes there's more than one soil mate out there for your lovelorn vegetable. Hopefully they don't all show up at once, otherwise a low-down dirty drama will ensue.

At the end of each perfect pairing you'll find a delicious **Recipe** that combines the best flavors and features of the happy couple. That way, you'll never again be at a loss for what to do with your abundant harvests!

Last but not least, in the back of the book is a section called **Garden Preparation, Planning & Care**. There you'll find even more detailed information about planting and maintenance, including bed building and container gardening, compost tips, natural pesticides and fertilizers, and crop rotation recommendations. Everything you need for matchmaking success!

Now let's meet our happy companions . . .

The Soil Mates

Tomato ♥

Basil

TOMATO is probably the most popular girl in the garden bed. Everyone loves her seductive round fruits, and her colorful hues go with everything. BASIL may be loose and lanky, but he's a force to be reckoned with. He tries to make up for his minor shortcomings by helping deter pesky fruit flies and disease from voluptuous Tomato. In fact, Basil makes Tomato so happy that all summer long she remains fertile and glowing, qualities that show in her flavor.

Love Match

Tomato and Basil have similar personalities and requirements—that's why they get along so well. Both like to be planted in late spring, safely after the last frost, and to stay warm and moist during the growing season. A layer of mulch and regular watering in dry weather will keep them happy. Make sure they have ample sunshine, which improves their moods and complexions.

Tomato can grow pretty wild, so it's best to cage her before she sprawls all over the place. (Don't worry, she doesn't mind.) You can also try tying her vines to a stake as she grows.

Tomato is particular about her appearance. Avoid watering her from above—she doesn't like her leafy hair to get wet (it causes unsightly black spots). Instead, soak from below, deeply and indiscreetly. If you smoke, wash your hands before fondling Tomato, for she abhors the odor and the bugs that stalk tobacco (this includes flowering tobacco, *Nicotiana*).

My Place or Yours? Basil is easy to grow from seed or as a seedling. Tomato likes to be planted horizontally; it gives her better footing (roots form along her main stem at the leaf nodes).

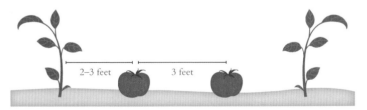

2–3 feet   3 feet

Plant basil at end of rows or around tomato cages.

Plant Profiles

Turn-Ons Not to sound naughty, but Basil likes to be pinched; otherwise he gets bitter. To keep his leaves tasting sweet, pinch off flowers before they bloom. (But leave a few for the bees!) For her part, vine-y Tomato likes to be caged to keep her tasty treats high and dry. There's nothing worse than rotten tomatoes.

Turn-Offs Tomato doesn't mix well with the Brassica family (cabbage, cauliflower, and their kin)—they all annoy one another and should be kept apart to avoid all-out garden drama.

Needy Alert If you haven't figured it out already, Tomato is a high-maintenance lady. She requires lots of compost; otherwise she'll wilt and withhold her precious fruits.

Stalker Alert Tomato is plagued by ferocious-looking hornworms, which chomp on her fancy foliage, mostly at night, when Basil is asleep. To attract the beneficial parasitic wasps whose larvae feed on their nasty host (they look like rice on the caterpillar's back), plant flowers that have umbrella- or daisy-like clusters, like tansy, dill, and clover.

Love Triangles Tomato likes to spread her love and is often unfaithful to poor Basil. She admires the tall stature of Asparagus and has an eye for Chives, Onion, Parsley, and Carrot. Basil is suspicious of all Tomato's crushes, but as long as they share the garden bed, her fantasies are fine. One of Basil's biggest threats is Garlic, which goes so well with Tomato—both in the bed and on the table. This tasty combo drives Basil mad!

Fried Tomato Caprese
Serves 4–6

Basil complements all veggies but is especially delicious when paired with tomatoes. Try this fresh salad composed of this match made in heaven.

Oil

4 tomatoes, cut into ⅓-inch rounds

Kosher salt and freshly ground black pepper

¾ c all-purpose flour

4 eggs

2 tbsp milk

1½ c panko bread crumbs

Pinch cayenne pepper

Pinch paprika

12 large basil leaves

1 ball fresh mozzarella (approx. 8 oz), drained and cut into ¼-inch slices

1. Preheat oven to 450°F. Heat oil in a frying pan over medium-high heat. Season tomatoes on both sides with salt and pepper.
2. Place flour in a shallow dish. In another shallow dish, beat eggs with milk. In another dish, mix bread crumbs with cayenne and paprika. Dredge tomatoes first in flour, then eggs, then bread crumbs.
3. Add only a few tomato slices to the pan at a time so that they cook evenly, about 2 to 3 minutes on each side. Place browned tomatoes on a baking sheet; top with fresh basil leaves and sliced mozzarella. Bake 10 minutes, or until cheese is melted and bubbly.

Cucumber ♥ Corn

With her tender skin—whether bumpy or smooth, pleated or pale—crispy CUCUMBER prefers to protect her delicate complexion by growing upward rather than lying on the ground. With his tall stature and regal bearing, CORN is especially desirable for this purpose. Cucumber is also sensitive to cold; fortunately, Corn is happy to cuddle. Intertwined together in their warm garden bed, this pair will flourish all season long.

Love Match

Both Cucumber and Corn love the heat of summer but detest being dry. Plant them when the soil is warm (60°F or above; about three weeks after your area's last frost date) and keep them well hydrated. Cucumber especially needs a steady supply of water to keep her liquidy insides happy. A layer of mulch helps retain moisture and keep their roots cool, too.

To be sure that Corn is feeling strong and sturdy enough to support Cucumber's long and many-tendriled vine, you may want to start him first. Cucumber is a fast grower and can usually be harvested within a couple months; she'll continue clinging to Corn's lanky stalks long after his cobs are gone. Corn requires a bit of patience and may take up to three months to produce his be-kerneled ears. When his silky golden hair turns brown, he's ready to be picked.

My Place or Yours? Cucumber likes a lumpy bed, and a square-foot raised hill made of compost and soil makes a perfect place to lay her head. In each hill, plant one or two cucumber seeds 1 foot apart. Plant Corn and his friends about 6 inches apart in a 6-foot-wide row or grid; thin to 1 foot. Cucumber will also help anchor Corn, who may wobble when the wind blows.

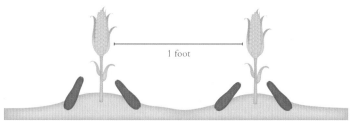

1 foot

Allow cucumber to clamber corn stalks.

Plant Profiles

Turn-Ons Cucumber is a diva about having her fruits picked, and she'll stop putting out if they're left on her vine. Harvest regularly, both the pickling and the slicing types. Corn loves his pollen to blow in the wind, so space rows about 6 feet apart to ensure good pollination.

Turn-Offs Cucumber dislikes Potato, with her bulbous figure and staring eyes. And not all types of corn get along: Varieties of sweet corns (hybrids) cannot be mixed, or cross-pollination will ruin their flavor. Stagger planting times or spread the types far and wide—at least 25 feet apart—to avoid cranky cobs.

Needy Alert Both plants demand good nutrition from super-rich soil. Corn's appetite for nitrogen seems insatiable, so feed a hearty helping of manure, fish emulsion, or compost all season long.

Stalker Alert To protect against the dreaded cucumber beetles, sow two or three Radish seeds in Cucumber's hills. Don't pull them out; just let them grow, even to seed, because Radish makes a good beetle repellent. Corn is plagued by evil borers that chomp their way through his delectable ears. The best defense is to eradicate the borer babies (larvae) by clearing away all stalks in the fall.

Love Triangles Cucumber is attracted to Beans, Peas, and Radish. So far she's resisted temptation, but Corn is always on guard.

Corn and Cuke Gazpacho
Serves 6

What better way for Corn and Cucumber to relax together than in a cool bath of tomato juice?

3 c tomato juice
2 tbsp extra-virgin olive oil
1½ c cooked sweet corn
   kernels
2 tomatoes, peeled and diced
1 red bell pepper, diced
1 cucumber, peeled, seeded,
   and diced

½ c fresh cilantro leaves
2 tbsp lemon juice
2 tbsp horseradish
1 tsp Worcestershire sauce
Kosher salt and freshly ground
   black pepper
6 celery stalks, halved
   lengthwise

1. Combine all ingredients except celery in a food processor. Pulse to desired chunkiness. Cover and refrigerate at least 2 hours. Serve chilled in bowls, each garnished with a celery stalk.

Beans ❤ Potato

Everyone knows that opposites attract. BEANS and POTATO are a perfect example. Although they look dissimilar, they get along splendidly. Beans is a slender guy who loves reaching for the sky. Potato is shy and firmly grounded. No shrinking violet, Beans always puts on quite a show. His eye-catching flowers are followed by sweet pods that are a gardener's delight. Meanwhile, humble Potato likes to hide in the ground, saving herself for later. Yet this dynamic duo is utterly devoted, generously protecting each other from pesky stalkers.

Love Match

Beans likes to tan under full sun but doesn't really care where (he's not too fussy about soil conditions). Potato is a low-maintenance lady, but, being a root vegetable, she cares where she sleeps. She prefers light sandy soil between her toes; heavy clay will cause her to pout and turn to mush.

Humble Potato likes to hide in the ground, and she takes a while to mature (3 to 4 months). Plant her 4 to 6 weeks before your area's last frost date, when the soil is workable but not wet. Despite being shy, she's pretty tough-skinned. Once she's ready to shine, her foliage will pop up, only to die back when she's fully grown. Her scrumptious spuds come in a range of colors, making for a color-filled root cellar.

Beans should hit the soil right after your area's last frost date to get a running start. Runner and pole types need a trellis or other support; bush types are usually fine on their own.

My Place or Yours? To grow Potato, first you need a good organic "seed" potato (not just one from the grocery store, which may not sprout). Cut it into pieces (about 3), making sure each has a few eyes. Dig trenches, nuzzle in one piece, and fill partway with soil. As foliage emerges, mound up more soil. This protects the potatoes from light, which turns them green (the green parts are poisonous). Plant beans on the sides of the potato hillock.

4 inches   4 inches

Once potatoes are about 6 inches tall, plant beans 4 inches apart alongside.

Plant Profiles

Turn-Ons Potato likes soil that's more acid than what most other veggies prefer, which Beans will tolerate for the sake of his sweetheart. As a legume, Beans does require a little special care: Before planting, dust his seeds with a bacterial inoculant. This helps him convert nitrogen from the air and improves soil fertility, to boot. Plus it's safe for organic use.

Turn-Offs Beans dislikes the whole Onion (Allium) family. He finds Onion lazy in his hygiene, what with his offensive smell and all. Beans also dislikes Fennel because of his odor and Basil, well, just because. Potato will never invite Cucumber, Pumpkin, Zucchini, Sunflower, Turnip, or Tomato to her garden party.

Needy Alert Beans is the lowest-maintenance companion; enjoy him while you can. Though not required for his happiness, a little compost halfway through the growing season will help the long-bearing pole types. Potato enjoys a good mulch dressing; straw is best.

Stalker Alert The Colorado potato beetle and the Mexican bean beetle are this pair's worst enemies. These nemeses may be hand-picked as soon as they rear their ugly heads.

Love Triangles Beans is attracted to Celery, with her curly hair and statuesque form. This is a sore subject for Potato, who is sensitive about her voluptuous figure. Beans also gets along with Cucumber and Corn, which complicates things if Corn and Cucumber are already in a relationship.

Indian Potatoes with Green Beans
Serves 4

Potato and Beans stew in their love in this aromatic dish.

1 tbsp olive oil
3 large garlic cloves, minced
2 tsp fresh ginger, peeled and minced
1 tsp turmeric
1 tsp ground coriander
1 tsp paprika
12 small red potatoes, cut or quartered into ½-inch chunks

3 lb fresh green beans, trimmed, washed, and snapped in two
3 c chicken or vegetable stock
4 tbsp unsalted butter, sliced
Kosher salt and freshly ground black pepper
¼ c fresh lemon juice
½ c fresh cilantro, chopped

1. Heat oil in a heavy skillet over medium heat; add garlic, ginger, turmeric, coriander, and paprika and cook 1 minute. Mix in potatoes and green beans, stir, and add stock. Cover and cook 6 minutes.
2. Uncover and increase heat to medium-high; add butter and cook until potatoes are tender and liquid is reduced to a glaze, about 10 minutes more. Season generously with salt and pepper and drizzle with lemon juice. Sprinkle with fresh cilantro and serve immediately.

Carrot ♥ Onion

Sugary CARROT finds well-built ONION exceedingly attractive, especially because his bulbous, intimidating rotundity (and repelling scent) is perfect for scaring off her corrosive stalker, the annoying carrot rust fly. In exchange, Carrot makes Onion look good by distracting others from his, um, smelliness (sorry, O!). Onion loves Carrot's ferny top and accepts her in any of her fancy forms, whether long and slender or short and stocky. He's a sucker for her sweetness.

Love Match

Carrot and Onion share many likes and dislikes, making them easy-care companions. They can tolerate a chill, so early-spring planting is possible for gardeners in cooler climes. Choose an exposed spot since both enjoy basking in the sun but want it all to themselves. They frown on uninvited guests, so pull weedy competition (gently!) before these have a chance to choke out your delicate root veggies.

As a seedling, Carrot has a hard time poking her head through crusty earth, so keep her bed moist. Too much water will cause her to rot, so moderation is the best policy. Fortunately, Onion can handle damp conditions—except after his top part turns brown and topples over. Then it's time to pull him up. Don't delay, especially if rain is forecast; once his bulbs are fully formed, too much moisture makes them mushy. Be sure to leave his tops on to dry. Braiding them makes for nice kitchen decoration.

My Place or Yours? The key to making Carrot happy is to give her lots of covers—loose 'n' fluffy well-draining soil that's dug deeply (to a depth of at least 10 inches), with compost added. Seeds can be sown directly from early spring through early fall (to overwinter). Onion can tolerate poor soil, though he too benefits from a well-prepared bed. He can be grown from seed but is usually planted in "sets" (transplants).

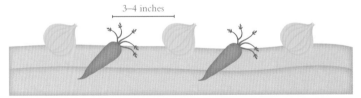

3–4 inches

Carrots and onions need only a little wiggling room, 3 to 4 inches all around.

Plant Profiles

Turn-Ons Once Carrot and Onion get growing, there's not much to do to keep them happy and productive. A moist weed-free bed is all they desire.

Turn-Offs Carrot hates Dill—she calls him "Dill weed" all the time. She also has a sour relationship with Apple. Don't store the two in the same room, or you'll end up with a bitter-tasting Carrot. Onion likes most other veggies, but they don't all like him. Beans, Peas, and Asparagus are among his detractors.

Needy Alert Carrot is a little fickle in her flavor, so make sure her bed is enriched with sufficient lime, humus, and potash to sweeten her disposition. Too much nitrogen or stifling heat can make her bitter. A little cold snap will have the opposite effect, enhancing her naturally sweet disposition.

Stalker Alert Onion's bug-repelling powers are well known in the garden world, and most pests leave him alone. Carrot relies on his strong scent to deter her archenemy, the carrot rust fly. Crop rotation usually helps keep Carrot fly-free too.

Love Triangles Carrot likes to hang out with her Salad Posse: Tomato, Lettuce, Beet, and Asparagus. Onion fits in with Carrot's peeps, especially Beet, but don't spread any ménage à trois rumors. He's not as fond of Carrot's weakness for buff Asparagus, so he never leaves them alone together. Onion's cousin Leek, plus his herb pals Rosemary and Sage, are Carrot's friends too, but their wimpy build poses no threat to rotund Mr. O.

Carrot and Onion Soup
Serves 4–6

Carrot is a sweetie, but warmed-up Onion has a sweet side too.

2 tbsp butter
1 tbsp olive oil
1 c diced onions
½ c diced celery
2 tbsp fresh ginger, minced
1 tbsp garlic, minced
½ lb carrots, peeled and
   roughly chopped

4–6 c chicken or vegetable
   stock
Kosher salt and freshly ground
   black pepper
1 bay leaf
½ c heavy cream
1 lime
Chopped chives, for garnish

1. Set a large stock pot over medium-high heat. Add butter and olive oil to the pot; once melted, add onions and celery. Cook vegetables until onions are translucent, about 3–4 minutes. Add ginger and garlic and cook 1 minute. Add carrots and continue cooking, stirring occasionally, until they are lightly caramelized and start to soften, about 7–8 minutes. Add stock, salt, pepper, and bay leaf to the pot and bring to a boil, then reduce to a simmer. Continue to cook until carrots are tender, about 20–25 minutes.

2. Remove bay leaf and puree the soup directly in the pot; alternatively, you can puree it in batches in a blender. Adjust seasoning if needed. Back in the pot, add heavy cream and stir to combine. Serve hot in bowls, garnishing with a squeeze of lime and a sprinkle of chives.

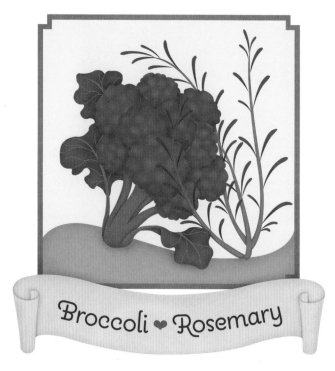

Broccoli ♥ Rosemary

Equipped with sensitive olfactory powers, floret-filled BROCCOLI (along with his whole Brassica family) is attracted to the perfume of aromatic herbs. Fluffy and fragrant, ROSEMARY is a sought-after lady in the vegetable patch and herb garden alike. Broccoli appreciates her ability to repel his archenemy, the cabbage moth, and admires her surprisingly strong, woody physique. She loves his sweet nutritious side. They may look like an odd couple, but don't be fooled. Many a gardener has caught them cuddling in the garden bed.

Love Match

The three keys to successfully growing Rosemary are sun, excellent drainage, and good air circulation—so don't crowd her. If you live in a frost-free area, she will happily grow in the ground year-round; in cooler climates, plant her in a pot and bring her in during winter. Once settled, she'll grow nice and stout, forming a 2- to 3-foot woody shrub in cooler areas and up to 6 feet in southerly regions. Broccoli comes in several varieties with sequential maturity dates, ensuring a summer-long forest of flavor-filled florets.

Your matchmaking efforts will be far more successful if you start both Broccoli and Rosemary as nursery-grown plants. (See "Mail-Order Brides," page 108, for more information.) In most gardens, it just takes too long for direct-sown seedlings to fill in.

My Place or Yours? Rosemary likes a sandy but well-draining soil (amend with compost to aid drainage) and 6 to 8 hours of full sunlight. Broccoli prefers a wealthy neighborhood, with rich soil containing lots of compost and manure. He's not a fan of extreme heat, a trait that his partner finds disappointing but does her best to downplay when he starts to sulk.

18–24 inches

Plant rosemary between (or in the middle of) a group of broccoli.

Plant Profiles

Turn-Ons Both plants love the sun, but Broccoli is a bit fussier during hot spells, which cause him to bolt (send up a flower stalk and go to seed). Plant him in early spring to be picked before the heat comes or in late summer for a fall harvest.

Turn-Offs Broccoli prefers not to see Tomato, Strawberry, or Beans in his vicinity. He dislikes the color red and just doesn't like the look of lanky legumes.

Needy Alert Broccoli has a pretty big appetite, so make sure to provide plenty of compost and manure a few weeks after planting. If you withhold nutrients and moisture, he may take revenge by allowing cavities (hollow parts) to form inside his stem. Holey Broccoli! It's a sad sight, indeed.

Stalker Alert In addition to his archnemesis, the cabbage moth, which lays its eggs in the soil under his canopy, Broccoli may be attacked by amorous aphids. You can protect him from their advances by applying garlic spray (see recipe, page 115) before his flowers bud. Ladybugs are a dear friend that will happily feast on pests. Also, Broccoli tends to attract a much larger stalker in the form of a furry fella called Rabbit. Move Onion into the neighborhood to scare off hungry hoppers.

Love Triangles Unfortunately, Broc is a little loose with his love and enjoys the company of Potato, Beet, and Onion. Rosemary is well aware of his "free love" philosophy, which runs in his family. To promote horticultural harmony, they have adopted a "don't ask, don't tell" approach to dealing with his indiscretions. It seems to work.

Cream of Broccoli Soup with Rosemary
Serves 6

Warm or cold, this soil-mate soup is a refreshing delight.

1 tsp butter
1 c white wine
2 medium yellow onions,
  coarsely chopped (2 c)
3 garlic cloves, slivered
½ lb celery, sliced
1¼ lb broccoli, heads cut
  into florets, stalks trimmed,
  peeled, and cubed

1 lb all-purpose potatoes,
  peeled and cubed
2 c low-fat milk
5 c chicken or vegetable stock
1 tbsp fresh rosemary, minced
⅛ tsp ground nutmeg
Kosher salt and freshly ground
  black pepper

1. In a large, heavy soup pot over medium-high heat, heat butter and wine to bubbling. Add onion and sweat 5 minutes, stirring frequently to prevent browning. Add garlic and cook an additional minute. Add celery, broccoli, and potato and sauté 5 more minutes, stirring frequently. Add milk and stock. Lower heat to medium and simmer 20 minutes, or until potato is cooked.

2. Let soup cool slightly and then transfer in batches to a blender and puree. Return soup to the pot and add rosemary, nutmeg, salt, and pepper. Heat through, taste for seasoning, and adjust if necessary.

Lettuce ♥ **Radish**

Lush and leafy, LETTUCE is a delightful girl to grow in the garden and is eaten more than any other veggie (but don't tell Tomato!). Smart and spicy, RADISH adds that extra zing to any occasion. These two laid-back crops are easily satisfied in the garden bed—happy to keep each other tender and succulent in cool weather, when most other vegetables, with their tender constitutions, are too wimpy to go outside. They're a pleasure to have at your veggie garden party. Plant them all around!

Love Match

$\mathcal{P}$erfect for the lazy gardener, Lettuce and Radish are easy to grow and happy to put out. They love to chill together in lower temps under a weaker sun, so the shorter days of early spring are prime growing time. Plant them as soon as the soil is workable but not wet. They can also be planted again in late summer, for a fall harvest. If you prepare the soil well and keep it moist, this dynamic duo shouldn't ask for more. Both come in a variety of colors, too—Lettuce in shades of garnet, olive green, and chartreuse; Radish in amethyst, yellow, and white (plus red, of course). Just think of the rainbow that awaits on your salad plate!

My Place or Yours? This companionable couple will grow in average soil that's on the chilly side, even as low as 45°F. They're also perfect candidates for containers (see "Pillow Pals," page 113, for pot-planting tips). Direct sow seeds about ⅛ inch deep for Lettuce and about ½ inch for Radish. Make successive plantings every 2 to 3 weeks for a continual harvest all season long.

2–3 inches   4–6 inches

Plant radish between lettuce, either in grids or in rows.

Plant Profiles

Turn-Ons Lettuce likes it when you "cut and come again," trimming her outer leaves to promote new ones. After 2 or 3 cuttings she'll become bitter, so pull the plants and start new ones.

Turn-Offs Radish is pretty friendly, but Lettuce has her complexes. She's particularly sensitive about Parsley, whose leafy hair is too haughty for Lettuce's tastes.

Needy Alert One word: Heat. Both need some SPF or they will overheat under a strong sun. They may show you their bitter displeasure by bolting and going directly to seed. Partial shade will keep these low-maintenance lovers cool and comfy. Try planting them under tall annuals (zinnias, cosmos, sunflowers) or tucked under broad-leaved veggies (broccoli, eggplant).

Stalker Alert Aphid attacks on lettuce can be deterred with a sharp blast of water from the garden hose; slugs can be hand-picked (ugh!), drowned in cups of soapy water placed at ground level, or trapped under boards. (Turn the boards over to give birds a squishy feast.) Radish's leaves might be riddled by flea beetle damage (he's often used as a trap crop for them; see page 117). Try offering a blanket (row cover) to keep his goods under wraps.

Love Triangles Lettuce also enjoys the company of Cucumber, Carrot, and Strawberry. Her attraction to Strawberry really aggravates Radish, who feels that Strawberry is a fruity outsider and doesn't deserve Lettuce's company. Though Radish will never admit it, he is attracted to Squash's curvy figure.

Lettuce Wraps
Serves 4–6

Lettuce loves wrapping her leaves around dashing Radish.

3 tbsp fresh lime juice
3 tbsp vegetable oil, divided
1 tbsp soy sauce, divided
1 tbsp fish sauce, divided
3 tsp grated fresh ginger
2 garlic cloves, minced
1 lb medium fresh shrimp, peeled, deveined, and chopped

1 head iceberg lettuce, cored, cut in half
½ red bell pepper, diced
2 green onions, sliced
1 bunch radishes, cleaned and sliced
½ c fresh cilantro, chopped

1. In a medium bowl, combine lime juice, 2 tablespoons oil, ½ tablespoon soy sauce, ½ tablespoon fish sauce, ginger, and garlic. Add shrimp and let marinate in refrigerator 30 minutes.
2. In a pan, heat remaining oil over medium-high heat. Add shrimp along with marinade and cook 3 minutes, or until shrimp are pink. Stir in remaining soy and fish sauces.
3. Separate lettuce into leaves. Spoon about ¼ cup mixture down the center of each lettuce leaf and top with bell pepper, green onion, radish, and cilantro. Wrap carefully, fold-side down. Serve immediately.

Spinach ♥ Pepper

Like most couples, SPINACH and PEPPER are a case of opposites attract. For starters, they have differing tastes when it comes to climate. Spinach prefers cool and moist conditions; Pepper likes warm soil and abundant sunshine (though not too much). Their compromise: Pepper considerately leans his leaves over Spinach, giving her the shade she needs to thrive, while Spinach helps shelter Pepper's fruits from the scorching sun. Though they may seem like an unorthodox couple, these soil mates are perfectly happy to get their roots entwined.

Love Match

Spinach is an early riser in the garden bed. She can be planted as soon as the soil can be worked in the spring, and seeing her nutritious dark-green leaves is a welcome sign of the growing season. Her seeds can even be broadcast over frozen ground or snow cover in late winter to germinate as the soil thaws. Spinach thinks practice makes perfect, so plant successive crops for several weeks to keep the harvest going until hot weather comes. Sow her seeds again in late summer for fall and early-winter harvests.

While Spinach is out in the cold, Pepper prefers to stay inside. The easiest way to get him growing is to start him from seed indoors during late winter and transplant him into the garden after the soil and air have warmed up. Although Spinach loves taller companions, her mate does have some unique tastes that she finds peculiar. For one thing, Pepper likes to cover his feet in sulphur when he's growing. She just looks away.

My Place or Yours? Sow 12 to 15 Spinach seeds for every foot, about ½ inch deep. When plants are 1 inch tall, thin to a spacing of 4 inches. (Rows may be as close as 1 foot.) Set Pepper transplants 12 to 18 inches apart.

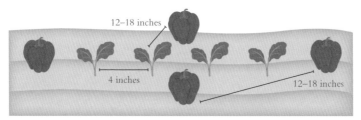

Plant peppers outside rows of spinach.

Plant Profiles

 Turn-Ons Like her leafy cousin Lettuce, Spinach adores the "cut and come again" approach to harvesting. She's also not a sun-worshiper, so tuck her in behind or under other plants to give her the SPF she needs when the summer heat kicks in.

Turn-Offs Keep in mind that Spinach doesn't get along with Potato, and Pepper dislikes Fennel.

Needy Alert Pepper is a fussy man. He cannot tolerate frost and hates cold wet soil. When temperatures dip below 50°F at night or soar above 90°F during the day, Pepper gets lazy and grows slowly. His leaves may turn yellow and his flowers could drop off in an alarming show of disdain.

Stalker Alert Pepper can't protect Spinach all the time. Fortunately, Radish has been known to give his life to protect her from the leafminer. His derring-do as a trap crop is celebrated throughout the veggie patch (see page 117 for more on his exploits).

Love Triangles As mentioned, Spinach likes tall plants. She's especially attracted to Beans and Peas, which doesn't sit well with Pepper. She claims he has nothing to worry about—she looks but doesn't touch. Spinach also finds Strawberry cute, but this low-grower is just too short. Being a member of Tomato's family, Pepper gets along with her nicely, and he's charmed by the dark and mysterious Eggplant as well.

Spinach and Pepper Couscous Loaf
Serves 4–6

Loafing around suits Spinach and Pepper just fine.

1 red bell pepper, diced	Kosher salt and freshly ground
½ large red onion, diced	black pepper
3 large garlic cloves, minced	3 c chicken or vegetable stock
2 tbsp olive oil	1½ c couscous
¼ c rice wine vinegar	2 c spinach leaves, chopped
½ tsp dried basil	1 c crumbled feta cheese
½ tsp dried oregano	1 large egg

1. Preheat oven to 325°F. Coat a 9-by-5-inch loaf pan with cooking spray and line with parchment paper, allowing paper to extend over the edges.
2. In a saucepan, sauté bell pepper, onion, and garlic in oil, stirring occasionally until onion is soft, about 6 minutes. Add vinegar, herbs, salt, and pepper and cook 1 minute. Stir in stock and bring to a boil. Stir in couscous and spinach; cover and remove from heat. Let stand 5 minutes and then fluff couscous lightly with a fork.
3. Combine cooled couscous mixture with feta and egg. Spoon mixture into the prepared pan, pressing firmly. Fold overhanging parchment over the top of the mixture. Bake 45 minutes, or until set. Cool 10 minutes; unfold parchment and invert loaf onto a platter. Cool 15 more minutes; slice and serve warm.

Celery

♥ Everyone

Happy-go-lucky CELERY gets along with most everyone. But she's also somewhat of a glutton whose demand for nutrient-rich soil is legendary. Not to mention constantly clamoring for water. Oh, and bolting if the weather changes. She's a handful, all right. Probably her best soil mates are gardeners watching their weight: Almost devoid of calories, she's still chock-full of vitamins and minerals. If you have the conditions to make her happy, try welcoming leggy and leafy Celery into your garden bed—and onto your dinner plate.

Love Match

Celery is a pretty demanding vegetable, but she's so crunchy and light and fun to hang out with, she just might be worth the effort. First off, her terms: She wants a long growing season (up to 5 months from seed!). She wants to be extremely well hydrated (she is 94% water, after all). She wants cooler temperatures (but not too cool or her hair will frizz). Wow! For busy gardeners, such a needy veggie can be a bit too much to handle.

But if you do decide to give her a chance, your best bet is to start seeds indoors and plant as soon as you can for a fall harvest. If you have boggy conditions, you may just be in luck; those are preferred. If not, water well and looong. She's a drinker!

If Celery's attributes aren't appealing enough to tempt you to plant her in your potager rather than pick her up at the store, consider her close relative, Celeriac. Easier to care for but a bit harder to find, this nutty-flavored root vegetable is a delicious alternative.

My Place or Yours? Start Celery seeds indoors, 8–10 weeks before your area's last frost date. Sow seeds ⅛ inch deep in sterile mix; transplant seedlings when soil temperatures stay between 55°F and 70°F—otherwise only your disappointment will grow, not your finicky fiber-filled stalks.

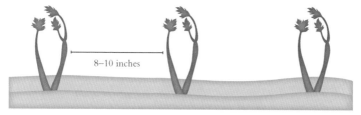

8–10 inches

Plant single file, 8 to 10 inches apart, in a 4-inch-deep trench.

Plant Profiles

Turn-Ons Where to start? There's the Cabbage family, her friends the salad greens, tall and tender Asparagus, her favorite couple Carrot and Onion, . . . You get the picture.

Turn-Offs Celery likes to take her time getting ready. She can't just be plopped right into the garden bed, you know. So start her as a seed indoors or buy her as a nursery-grown seedling. When she's about 4 inches tall, set seedlings outdoors to acclimate to the cooler temperatures for a couple weeks (known as "hardening off").

Needy Alert Celery's a heavy drinker, but she can handle her liquid. Make sure she gets lots of water throughout her long growing period. She also likes sun but not too much heat, which makes her bolt and toughen up. No one likes hard stalks.

Stalker Alert Celery worms break her heart—literally. They burrow right in and make themselves at home in her tender core. You can pick them off, but remember that these unattractive pests will eventually transform into the beautiful black swallowtail butterfly. You just might want to sacrifice some of your crop rather than destroy this summer delight.

Love Triangles Love pentagons is more like it. Celery just loves everyone, and that can create a bit of tension in the garden bed. If you insist on forcing her to settle down, match her with a patient vegetable like Cauliflower. He understands that even though Celery claims he's her "soil mate," she still maintains a lot of "friends."

Oven-Roasted Celery & Cauliflower
Serves 4–6

Celery is not the tasteless hussy you may have thought. With the right accessories and herbs, she can be a flavorful veggie that keeps you guessing.

1 head cauliflower (about 2 lb), cut into bite-size florets (about 8 c)
4 celery stalks, sliced
½ c extra-virgin olive oil
10 garlic cloves, roughly chopped or sliced
1 tbsp fresh lemon juice
¼ tsp crushed red pepper
Kosher salt and freshly ground black pepper
2 tsp roughly chopped fresh thyme leaves

1. Preheat oven to 450°F.
2. Toss all ingredients together. Spread on a baking sheet and roast until golden brown and tender, about 25 minutes.

Peas ❤ Turnip

PEAS and TURNIP met in the early-spring garden and have been soil mates ever since. Cool, calm, and collected, they soon noticed how mutually beneficial their relationship was. Being a shy retiring type, Turnip appreciates the way Peas lets it all hang out. While Peas soaks up the sun above, Turnip's leafy tops shade the soil around her mate's roots, which add a nice dose of nitrogen to the soil. They fit together nicely, each getting the light it needs without invading the other's personal space.

Love Match

Quick and easy to grow, Peas and Turnip are a garden favorite. They give a welcome early harvest (maturing in about 45–60 days) and then graciously make way for summer-loving crops. (Peas can be planted later for a fall harvest, too.) Both can be direct sown, and the perfect time is a few weeks before your area's last frost date. The sooner the better for Peas, who tends to get cranky as the temperature cranks up. He's pretty much down for the count by summertime. Till then, the key word is *harvest*: Keep picking his pods or he'll stop producing.

Peas comes in a several forms: shelling, snap, snow, and even the ooh-la-la French kind called *petits pois*. They vary in height (vine vs. bush types) and harvests, though overall Peas isn't a big producer. But, like Turnip, you may have a sweet spot for his sugary treats, which make him worthwhile. Turnip has a couple colors up her sleeve too, as well as a tasty lesser-known relative called Rutabaga. Turnip is ready to harvest when she's about 2 or 3 inches around.

My Place or Yours? Peas has a friendly family and can be planted just 1 to 2 inches apart in rows about 2 feet apart. He may need a trellis or more rustic support made of brush. Sow Turnip 2 inches apart, in rows 12 to 16 inches apart. She can get a little overzealous, so you may need to thin her seedlings to 6 inches. (Eat the greens in a salad or sauté.)

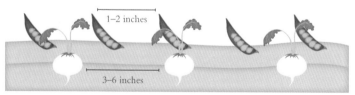

Plant turnips in front of or alongside a row of peas.

Plant Profiles

Turn-Ons Like his leguminous brother Beans, Peas needs a little help before getting into the garden bed. Dip his seeds in an inoculant, which helps improve his yield. He and Turnip are happy in a variety of soil types as long as drainage is good, and they love to bask in the sunshine.

Turn-Offs Peas has a sensitive nose, so don't plant him near Garlic or Onion. Their strong odors can turn sweet Pea into a sourpuss. Also, Peas and Turnip dislike Potato. It's a long scandalous story . . . Let's not get into it.

Needy Alert Turnip prefers deeply worked soil for her tender roots, with a little compost thrown in to keep her cravings satisfied. Peas isn't too particular about his soil, but does appreciate a side dressing of compost and bonemeal to keep him healthy and productive.

Stalker Alert Peas and Turnip have few insect stalkers to ruin the mood. Diligent crop rotation is usually enough to foil any foes.

Love Triangles This is a sensitive subject for Turnip, especially after the whole Potato affair. Peas enjoys the company of Carrots, Radish, Cucumber, and Beans. Though Radish and Turnip are cousins (both are in the Cabbage family), Turnip doesn't think Radish is a good influence on Peas; she blames him for Peas' indiscretions.

Turnip Bake with Fresh Peas
Serves 4–6

A quick and easy casserole that's sure to "peas"!

4 lb turnips, peeled and cut
    into 1-inch chunks
1 c whole milk
6 tbsp salted butter
2 tbsp extra-virgin olive oil,
    plus more for drizzling
6 tbsp unsalted butter
½ large onion, diced

Pinch sugar
Zest and juice of 1 lemon
1 lb fresh shelled peas
Kosher salt and freshly ground
    black pepper
¼ c roughly chopped flat-leaf
    parsley
½ c grated Parmesan

1. Preheat oven to 425°F. Place turnips in a saucepan with enough water to cover. Bring to a boil and simmer, covered, until easily pierced with a knife, about 35 minutes. Drain. In a separate saucepan, heat milk and salted butter over low heat until butter has melted and milk begins to simmer.

2. Puree turnips in several batches in a food processor. With the motor running, add milk mixture in a steady stream until turnips are smooth. Transfer to a casserole dish.

3. Heat olive oil with unsalted butter in a medium saucepan over medium heat. Add onion, sugar, and lemon juice and cook until onions are browned, 5–6 minutes. Add peas and lemon zest and continue cooking until peas are hot; season with salt and pepper.

4. Pour peas and onion mixture over turnips in casserole, drizzle with extra-virgin olive oil, and sprinkle parsley and Parmesan overtop. Bake 25 minutes, or until lightly browned.

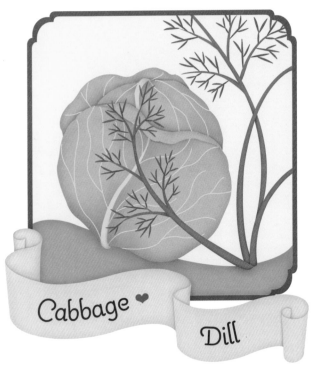

Cabbage ♥ Dill

Easy-to-grow CABBAGE and DILL are a perfect match, though it may be somewhat one-sided. Sluggish Cabbage is able to take her time getting ready while daring Dill scares away stalkers, attracting beneficial insects and giving his sweetheart's growth a boost. He keeps her mood happy and her health snappy by acting as host to a party of predatory wasps, which eat the bugs bugging his spherical soil mate. Though Cabbage may be fickle, she keeps Dill happy too. Some may call him smelly, but she stands by her man.

Love Match

Not a Southern belle by nature, Cabbage does not enjoy summer's intensity, preferring to attend garden parties in spring and fall. Don't get her wrong, though—she still needs full sun and fertile soil, just not the sweltering heat. She likes to be planted either very early, to mature before blazing days and heavy humidity arrive, or later in summer, to be ready for fall. Fall is also when there are fewer annoying pests to attack her beautiful balls of tightly packed leaves. In climates with moderate temps and uniform moisture, Cabbage will grow year-round. Harvest her when she's fully formed but still firm.

Dill's feathery frosty blue-green foliage and dainty yellow flower-umbrellas stand tall all summer long. Once he's happily settled in, he'll reward you by sowing himself throughout your veggie patch. His leaves and seeds are edible and decorative, adding a pungent note to dishes or an airy touch to bouquets.

My Place or Yours? Start Cabbage seeds indoors, about 8 weeks before your area's last frost. Plant them 10 to 12 inches apart in an alternating (checkerboard) pattern. Dill is all about randomness and chance—scatter his seeds and cover lightly with soil. Once he gets growing, thin to 6 or 12 inches apart.

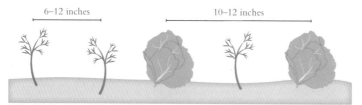

Sprinkle dill seeds randomly around cabbage seedlings.

Plant Profiles

Turn-Ons Cabbage has a healthy appetite—rich soil is her desire—and she enjoys a good aphrodisiac in the form of organic matter. But not too much or she'll split (literally). Dill takes off in full sun and well-drained soil but is otherwise not picky about his surroundings. He'll usually seed in anywhere he feels comfy.

Turn-Offs Cabbage dislikes Strawberry and her friends, Pepper, Eggplant, and Grapes. Dill doesn't mind them much but has banned a few of his own rivals from the garden bed, including Carrot and Caraway.

Needy Alert Cabbage can tolerate a lot of things, but bad drainage is not one of them. Watering steadily is a must, but not so much that she rots. She's also fickle about her ideal temperature. If she isn't behaving in spring, try planting her in summer for a fall harvest.

Stalker Alert The beleaguered Brassica family—including Broccoli, Brussels Sprouts, and Cabbage—are all stalked by the same nefarious worms, loopers, and maggots. Crop rotation or a row cover is your best defense.

Love Triangles Cabbage has a thing for aromatic herbs and veggies, which drives Dill crazy. She's attracted to Onion and Spinach and is friends with Celery, Beets, Chamomile, and Chard. Everyone gets along though, especially with Dill's best friends, Lettuce and Squash. Cabbage and Dill also like to double-date with Cucumber and Corn.

Braised Cabbage with Fresh Dill
Serves 4–6

Just like in their relationship, Cabbage needs a little time to get soft and delicious, while always-fresh Dill is ready in an instant.

1 tbsp sherry
1 large cabbage, quartered, cored, leaves separated and torn into large pieces
2 tbsp butter

2 tbsp olive oil
2 tbsp chopped fresh dill
½ bunch fresh chives, chopped
Kosher salt and freshly ground black pepper

1. Bring a big pot of water to a boil over high heat; add 3 tbsp salt. Add sherry, then cabbage, and boil over high heat until cabbage is wilted, 2–3 minutes. Drain. Mix in a bowl with butter, oil, dill, chives, and salt and pepper to taste.

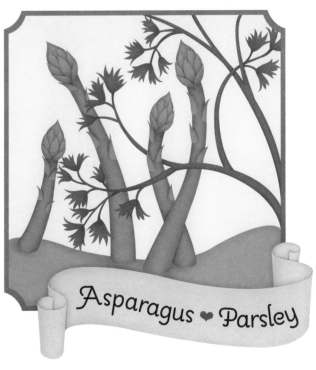

Asparagus ♥ Parsley

Patient PARSLEY is the perfect partner for tender and bashful ASPARAGUS. Her beautiful hair distracts the asparagus beetle from nibbling on her mate's sweet spears, and she attracts predatory wasps that further protect him from harm. Though Asparagus doesn't do much for Parsley, his tall towering physique is enough to keep her satisfied. He may not show his affection all the time, but Parsley knows that her Asparagus is a softy at heart.

Love Match

Asparagus requires a patient soil mate as well as a patient gardener, but the investment always pays off. Even though his tempting spears cannot be harvested the first few years, once he's had time to settle in, he'll become a perennial favorite, poking up year after year. In fact, hardy Asparagus has been known to show up at garden parties for decades. Such a tasty long-lasting return is well worth the effort.

To ensure his comfort, provide a double-dug bed (see "Tilling Tips," page 101) amended with organic matter, good drainage, and 6 hours of full sun per day. After 3 years, you can begin to harvest, either by cutting or by snapping off the spears at ground level. Take only those thicker than a pencil and about 8 inches tall, leaving the thin ones to grow. Their bushy ferny form is a nice accent in the fall garden.

Parsley is pretty adaptable to Asparagus's ways. She can grow in full sun or light shade and, as a hardy biennial, often survives winter too, when she will kindly keep watch over her slumbering mate.

My Place or Yours? Asparagus is usually grown from year-old roots, called "crowns." Dig 6-inch-deep trenches. Shape soil into a mound and spread crowns overtop; plant 15 inches apart in wide rows. Sow Parsley indoors, since seeds can take 3 to 4 weeks to germinate. Plant in early spring.

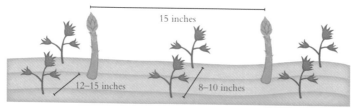

15 inches

12–15 inches   8–10 inches

Plant parsley around asparagus in rows at least 3 feet wide.

Plant Profiles

Turn-Ons Parsley and Asparagus are a pretty laid-back couple. After the initial care for his planting, Asparagus is happy to produce without much incentive—perhaps a topdressing of compost each spring. Parsley, too.

Turn-Offs This happy couple keeps to themselves and has few enemies. That said, if he can help it, Asparagus usually avoids Onion and Potato, who may encroach on his root space.

Needy Alert Although satisfied in the relationship, Asparagus does request a topping of a little aphrodisiac to keep him happy. Fertilize him with a coat of compost in early spring and after harvesting.

Stalker Alert Parsley can be attacked by creepy-crawly caterpillars, but these same pests will later transform into beautiful butterflies. She's a handy and sought-after host plant, so you may want to sacrifice some of your crop to these summer sylphs. Asparagus beetles are well controlled by picking them off. Some gardeners drown them in a dish of soapy water.

Love Triangles It's not really a love triangle—more of a soft spot: Both Parsley and Asparagus are pretty fond of Tomato. (Tomatoes contain a substance called solanine that deters the asparagus beetle.) Though Asparagus likes to hang out near Tomato's buxom fruits, Parsley is confident that her ferny foliage will always keep him firmly on her side of the garden bed.

Grilled Asparagus with Parsley Marinade
Serves 4–6

Behind every good veggie is an even better soil mate. In this dish, fresh-tasting Parsley complements mild-mannered Asparagus. The results are delicious!

3 tbsp minced fresh parsley
2 tbsp fresh lemon juice
¼ c olive oil
¼ tsp dry mustard

Kosher salt and freshly ground
 black pepper
1 lb fresh asparagus, trimmed
 and peeled

1. Preheat a grill. Place all ingredients except asparagus in a plastic zip-top bag and shake to mix thoroughly. Add asparagus and turn spears until coated. Let sit 30 minutes.
2. Grill asparagus 5 minutes over the hot grill. Every minute or so, roll each spear a quarter turn. Asparagus should begin to brown in spots (indicating that the natural sugars are caramelizing) but should not be allowed to char. *Note:* Dripping oil may cause flare-ups. Keep a spray bottle or glass of water handy to spritz coals, if necessary. Remove spears from grill and serve immediately.

Beet

♥ Mint

As the saying goes, still waters run deep, and that's especially true of BEET, who's content in her little corner of the garden bed. Her deep-reaching taproot gives her firm footing, so once she sets down roots she's there to stay for the season. MINT, meanwhile, is all over the place. His effusive personality can be hard to contain. But Beet— with her bright disposition and cheery color—just lets Mint roam. She knows he'll always be there when she needs him.

Love Match

Both Beet and Mint will tolerate a bit of shade, so it's easy to tuck them into a less-than-sunny spot. In fact, Beet doesn't like too much heat, so if temperatures rise above 85°F, she'll need to cool her roots. A layer of compost should do the trick. They both adore moisture too, so water with impunity.

Despite her delicate composition, Beet is a hardy girl. As a seedling she can withstand a touch of frost, so you can plant her early in the growing season. Harvest when she's about 3 inches in diameter. She's also a selfless veggie—even if she doesn't get eaten, she can be a great asset to your compost heap, adding magnesium as her leaves decompose.

Mint can be a fresh character (but in a good way). A wee bit overzealous, he wants room to roam and may grow out of control, crowding out poor little Beet. The good news is that you can easily contain him in a pot. Otherwise, he may well take over your entire garden!

My Place or Yours? Direct sow Beet seeds 1 to 4 weeks before your area's last frost, 1 inch deep, 4 inches apart, in all directions. Mint should be grown from seedlings and planted in early spring. Usually one plant is enough, but if you want more, space them 18 to 24 inches apart.

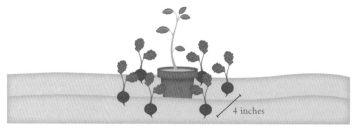

4 inches

Mint planted in a container will be easier to control.

Plant Profiles

Turn-Ons Like her friend Lettuce, Beet enjoys the "cut and come again" haircut. Just snip her outer leaves and pop them into salads or sautés—she's happy to oblige. Mint also likes a good pinching. Snipping back his leaves will promote a bushier growth habit.

Turn-Offs Beet and Beans don't get along really well; they always seem depressed around each other, which shows in their stunted growth. Keep the garden "upbeet" by keeping them apart.

Needy Alert Easygoing Beet hates to be demanding, but she really needs moisture, especially as a delicate seedling. A nice dressing of compost is welcome, helping to keep moisture in and weeds down and out. Like her comrades in roots, competition for nutrients will cause her to sulk and wilt.

Stalker Alert Mint is not exactly selfless, but he does ward off an array of pests, including mice and flea beetles, and attracts beneficial predatory wasps. He usually achieves this power through his strong fragrance. Beet is thankful for her mate's fragrant generosity.

Love Triangles Beet gets along with her root cousins Onion and Carrot, as well as the salad matriarch, Lettuce. Mint doesn't mind Beet's friends because he's usually busy with his own, namely Cabbage and Tomato.

Minty Beet Ice Cream
Makes about 2 quarts

Beet easily tames her wandering mate with this deliciously cool treat.

4 lb red beets	12 egg yolks
2 c milk	6 c cream
3 c sugar	½ c fresh mint, finely chopped

1. Wash beets thoroughly. (You can remove outer skin with a vegetable peeler if you prefer.) Cut into small pieces and run through a juicer. If you don't have a juicer, use a blender and strain the juice several times through cheesecloth to remove all the pulp.
2. Simmer juice 2 hours, until reduced by two-thirds. You should end up with about 4½ cups of liquid. Set aside to cool.
3. In a separate pot, combine milk and sugar and bring to a boil. Add a small amount of the hot milk to the eggs to temper them, stirring vigorously. Add a little more hot milk, still stirring vigorously, and then carefully stir the egg mixture into the pot. Add cream, beet juice, and fresh mint. Freeze according to the instructions for your ice-cream machine.

Summer Squash

❤ Borage

With their yellow-and-purple color scheme, the complementary couple of SQUASH and BORAGE is one of the garden's most attractive soil mates. They're much sought-after for double dates all summer long. Borage is a great partner. His handsome starry blossoms attract bees and predatory insects that help protect his many friends from pesky stalkers and dreaded diseases. Those are just a couple reasons why Squash is so smitten. Borage doesn't mind doing most of the work in their relationship. He's happy just to find a veggie who truly appreciates him.

Love Match

Squash comes from a big family of different shapes and sizes (including patty pan, butternut, acorn, and zucchini). So she often feels the need to stand out and can be a bit of a diva. She insists on making a grand garden entrance and won't show up until the soil has reached a perfect 75°F. She will only move into a wealthy neighborhood, so enrich her bed with compost or manure before planting. But when she's finally ready to make her warm-weather debut, watch out: She loves to spread out all over the place and let her fruits hang out in full sun.

Borage is of sturdier stock and way more easygoing. He doesn't mind being planted earlier, just after the last frost date, and likes the same conditions as his mate. He's a friendly repeat visitor to the garden; when you plant him once, he'll seed in and keep showing up year after year. Borage is helpful even after he's been discarded. In fact, he's as great an asset in the compost heap as he is in the raised bed.

My Place or Yours? Plant Squash 12 inches apart in a single row; thin seedlings to 2 to 3 feet apart. Sow Borage seeds just below the surface of the soil, thinning to at least 1 foot apart.

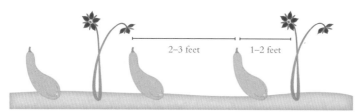

Intersperse borage between squash vines or at end of rows.

Plant Profiles

 Turn-Ons Well-watered and weed-free, that's all S and B need!

Turn-Offs Borage is a friend to many veggies, and his popularity is due to his selfless giving. Thanks to him, the soil around his friends becomes enriched with important minerals, like potassium and calcium. Squash occasionally fights with Potato, so keep them separated in the garden bed.

Needy Alert No needy mates here. This lackadaisical couple doesn't require aphrodisiacs (fertilizers). If you find they're being too prolific, you can harvest their flowers, both of which are delicious. Squash blossoms are tasty fried, and borage blooms taste like cucumber—a delightful addition to a summer salad.

Stalker Alert Squash can be prickly (especially her leaves), but it's understandable when you meet the mean bugs, beetles, and borers that bother her. She also hates being too damp, and her hair may develop a dandruff. You can treat this powdery mildew, and other types of wilt and rot that plague Squashy, with a natural spray (see page 116).

Love Triangles Squash used to date Corn, Radish, and Basil in seedling school, and they remain good friends. She still has a crush on Nasturtium, whose squash-bug-repelling qualities make Borage a wee bit envious. Borage has many friends, but they're all platonic. And with Borage seedlings popping up all over the place, there's plenty of his love to go around. Squash has nothing to worry about.

Summer Squash and Borage Fritters
Serves 4–6

These soil mates don't mind getting hot and bothered on a skillet to make this scrumptious dish.

4 eggs
1 c flour
4 tsp baking powder
½ c grated Asiago cheese
Kosher salt and freshly ground
  black pepper

1 bunch borage leaves,
  cut into strips
2 summer squash, grated
Extra-virgin olive oil,
  for frying

1. Combine eggs, flour, baking powder, 1½ cups of water, cheese, salt, and pepper in a bowl and whisk well to combine. Cover mixture and allow it to rest 2 hours.
2. In a tall heavy-bottomed pot, heat oil to 350°F. Stir borage and squash into the batter. Drop batter by spoonfuls into the hot oil and fry until golden brown. Remove from oil and set on a plate lined with paper towels to drain. Sprinkle with salt and serve immediately.

Eggplant

♥ Marigold

EGGPLANT is one the most striking veggies in the garden. But her voluptuous figure wasn't the first thing MARIGOLD noticed—it was the beautiful blossoms that preceded her jaw-dropping appearance. Though he's not as dark and mysterious as his mate, Marigold is no slouch, either. In fact, he's often called the Superman of the garden. His scented blossoms and good-looking root structure are the envy of all the other plants, though no one holds a grudge. They all welcome him with open leaves and hope he settles in next door.

Love Match

The gorgeous figure and flawless skin of Eggplant is not low maintenance. She is a sun worshiper who needs well-drained soil to flourish. But once she takes off, in a couple months she'll produce loads of sleek, delectable fruits on sturdy 2- to 3-foot-tall bushy plants. Though her offerings may be tantalizing, don't yank them off her arms; instead, snip them carefully and she'll happily provide more.

Marigold also likes full sun and well-drained soil—that's how he and Eggie met. Quick to bloom and easy to grow, he is a social flower that can (and should!) be planted freely around the garden. When grown from seed, he reaches stately heights and adds extra-special charm to both the veggie patch and the perennial border. His many varieties come in a range of summery colors and diverse flower forms that fit in anywhere.

My Place or Yours? Start Eggplant indoors 4 to 8 weeks before your area's last frost date. Place seedlings outside 2 weeks past the last frost date; space 15 inches apart in two rows. Plant Marigold at the same time, sprinkling seeds here and there and covering them lightly with soil.

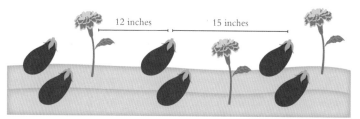

Plant marigold freely around eggplant.

Plant Profiles

Turn-Ons Marigold is amazingly altruistic, but he has his vain side, too. He always wants to look his best, so deadheading is necessary to keep him happy. "Deadheading" sounds bad but it's really not—in fact, lots of plants love it. Just snap off his spent blooms to make sure he keeps looking like the lady-killer he is at heart.

Turn-Offs Eggplant abhors Fennel, whose scent offends her delicate sensibilities. Marigold is a lover, not a fighter, but he does his best to keep Fennel out of sight.

Needy Alert Eggplant has a fertilizer addiction, and her favorite vice is fish emulsion. She should be sprayed monthly to keep her cravings satisfied. Eventually she'll enroll in a recovery program, but for now . . . just be an enabler.

Stalker Alert Eggplant's gorgeous appearance is bound to attract stalkers, so Marigold is always on guard. Eggplant also does charity work by volunteering as a trap crop to protect the Brassica family from annoying beetles (see page 117 for more on the heroism of trap crops).

Love Triangles Eggplant likes to hang out with her cousin Tomato, so they can gossip about the other veggies. Marigold can't help that he loves being friends with Basil, Beans, Cabbage, and Cucumber. He's had flings with many veggies, including Tomato, though Eggplant is completely unaware of this clandestine relationship.

Roasted Eggplant Spread
with Marigold Petals
Serves 4–6

Eggplant's smooth complexion is a perfect complement to this silky spread. Not to be upstaged, Marigold readily provides petals, making this flavorful concoction complete.

2 medium eggplants, peeled
  and cubed
1 red bell pepper, seeded
  and cubed
1 red onion, peeled and cubed
2 garlic cloves, minced
3 tbsp extra virgin olive oil

½ tsp cayenne pepper
Kosher salt and freshly ground
  black pepper
2 tbsp lemon juice
2 tbsp tahini
3 tbsp chopped marigold
  petals, plus extra for garnish

1. Preheat oven to 400°F. Toss eggplant, bell pepper, and onion in a large bowl with garlic, olive oil, cayenne, salt, and pepper. Spread mixture on a baking sheet. Roast 45 minutes, tossing once, until vegetables are lightly browned and soft. Allow to cool slightly.
2. Place vegetables in a food processor, add lemon juice and tahini, and pulse 3 or 4 times to blend. Season with salt and pepper. Transfer to a bowl and mix in marigold petals. Garnish with extra petals. Serve on veggies, crackers, or pita bread.

Pumpkin

♥ Sunflower

Nothing says happiness like sunny SUNFLOWER, all bright and cheery. He's a perfect foil for the sometimes-grumpy always-lumpy PUMPKIN. Sunflower doesn't mind that Pumpkin hogs all the space; he allows her to ramble around his feet while he shops for sun for the both of them. Sunflower is definitely the "giver" in the couple, improving soil and attracting beneficial insects, like predatory wasps, dainty lacewings, and pollinating bees. Pumpkin occasionally gives Sunflower root massages to show her appreciation.

Love Match

$\mathcal{P}$umpkin is a fun addition to the veggie bed, though she requires a bit of patience from the gardener. She takes a long time to get ready (about 100 days to harvest), so it's best to start her seeds indoors a few weeks before your area's last frost. She's sensitive to the cold at first, so harden off seedlings outdoors to improve your chances of soil-mate success. Pumpkin also likes rich soil, so a hefty dose of fertilizer or compost is necessary before settling her into bed.

Sunflower is a lot less needy than Pumpkin—he is, after all, "above" it all. His seeds can be sown directly in the garden bed about the same time as Pumpkin's seedlings are planted. Just beware of birds, which love to feed on Sunny's seeds. To deter these airborne snack-seekers, place a screen over new plantings; remove it once the sprouts poke through the soil.

My Place or Yours? To plant Pumpkin seedlings, dig a 3-foot-diameter hole and mix well-rotted compost or manure into the removed soil. Replace soil, creating a hill. Plant 2 or 3 seedlings at least 3 feet apart. Plant Sunflower seeds shallowly, just below the surface, about 6 inches apart; thin to 1 foot apart.

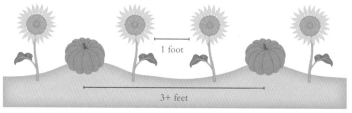

1 foot

3+ feet

Plant sunflower around pumpkin hills, in full sun.

Plant Profiles

Turn-Ons Both of these sun worshipers get sad in shade. If conditions are right, though, they'll thrive all growing season until a hard frost nips at their heels.

Turn-Offs Neither Sunflower nor Pumpkin care for Potato, who (they feel) sucks all the fun out of garden parties and stunts their growth. Pumpkin doesn't like Rosemary or Tomato, either. Sunflower doesn't like to be around pole Beans, who competes for all the attention, not to mention the sun and space.

Needy Alert Pumpkin can be a bit needy. She likes fertile soil (enrich her bed with compost before planting) and has a heavy appetite. Feed her a monthly serving of fish emulsion or compost to keep her satisfied. Not one to fuss too much, Sunflower may need some help staying upright in windy weather. He claims his unbalanced stature is genetic, but Pumpkin suspects he's been dipping into the fermented fish emulsion when she's not looking.

Stalker Alert Part of the Cucurbita family, Pumpkin suffers from attacks by squash bugs and cucumber beetles. Good crop rotation will help confuse these hungry harassers.

Love Triangles Both Sunflower and Pumpkin have carried on a relationship with Corn and Cucumber. This ménage à quatre allows them to socialize without wandering outside the garden bed.

Pumpkin Chutney with Sunflower Seeds & Dried Cranberries

Serves 4–6

Pumpkin may be a bit high-maintenance, but she becomes a sweetie when cooked to perfection, with her main man Sunny's seeds by her side.

1 lb pumpkin flesh, diced into ½-inch cubes	½ c brown sugar
2 tbsp extra-virgin olive oil	½ c apricot jam
½ large sweet onion	1 tsp ground cinnamon
1 clove garlic, minced	½ tsp ground nutmeg
3 tbsp cider vinegar	½ c raw sunflower seeds
3 slices fresh ginger	1 c dried cranberries
Dash cayenne pepper	¼ tsp ground allspice
1 tsp ground mustard	1 lemon, juiced
	1 whole red chile pepper

1. Place all ingredients in a pot and cook slowly over low heat until thick, about 1–2 hours. Remove and discard chile pepper. Serve immediately or transfer to a jar and refrigerate.

Zucchini ♥ Nasturtium

Overzealous ZUCCHINI has been known to crash one too many garden parties. If you're not careful, he could easily take over your whole garden bed. Fortunately, he's complemented by mild-mannered NASTURTIUM. Her vining stem loves twining up other plants, and her rambling habit provides sought-after shelter for beneficial ground beetles and spiders, who just love lounging under her cool umbrella-shaped leaves. This rampant but relaxed couple is sure to make a great addition to any veggie garden.

Love Match

$\mathcal{F}$ast-paced and fast-growing, Zucchini may just start showing up on your dinner plate less than two months after planting. Despite his minor quirks (vigorous production that's hard to stay on top of), he's a great asset to the gardener, not least for all the vitamins and flavor packed into his compact fruit. He's also super easy to grow, as is his mate, the dainty and delightful Nasturtium.

Although her nickname may be "Nasty," this cheerful little plant is anything but. Everyone wants to be her friend because of all the hard work she does in the garden. Gardeners love her too for her edibility—both her slightly peppery leaves and her mild-flavored flowers. Laid-back and always ready with a welcoming upturned blossom, Nasturtium doesn't require much to enjoy herself, even faring well in dry, poor soil. She makes an excellent ground cover, so let her drift and trail anywhere she likes. She'll happily create a colorful coverlet for your garden bed.

My Place or Yours? Plant Zucchini in full sun when the soil is a warm 75°F. Mix compost or manure into soil and plant seeds 1 inch deep, 2 to 3 feet apart. Plant Nasturtium after your area's last frost date, ½ inch deep and a foot apart.

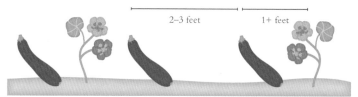

2–3 feet   1+ feet

Plant nasturtium around zucchini and anywhere you'd like to gracefully cover the soil.

Plant Profiles

Turn-Ons Zucchini is another of those plants that likes to be picked—whether you pluck his fruits or his blossoms, he doesn't mind a bit. A big Zucchini is a bad Zucchini, so harvest when the fruit is no more than 8 inches long (the smaller, the tastier). The blossoms are edible too—perfect for frying, stuffing, and sautéing.

Turn-Offs Easygoing and easy to grow, Zucchini and Nasturtium get along with most guests who show up in their garden bed . . . except Potato. They wonder what she's up to, hidden underground like that. (If they only knew.)

Needy Alert Content in their relationship, Zucchini and Nasturtium don't usually clamor for compost or other aphrodisiacs to keep them growing.

Stalker Alert She may look pretty and polite, but plucky Nasturtium is one courageous crop. She bravely lures obnoxious aphids away from other plants (see page 118 for more on her trap-crop exploits). Zucchini can fall victim to assaults by various types of powdery mildew, which will cause him to wilt and whimper. Try a baking-soda spray to perk him up (see page 116 for natural pesticides).

Love Triangles Zucchini and his Squash family have been friends with Corn, Beans, Cucumbers, Radish, Marigold, and Basil ever since they all moved into the same neighborhood. Nasturtium realizes that her mate is a social butterfly and accepts all his colorful friends.

Zucchini Custard with Nasturtiums
Serves 4–6

This delectable dish keeps prolific Zucchini occupied while lovely Nasturtium lends her petals, for that extra touch of beauty.

4 tbsp butter
2 lb zucchini, diced
3 eggs
½ c light cream
2 tbsp bread crumbs
½ c diced onion

1 tsp Worcestershire sauce
Dash hot sauce
Kosher salt
¼ c grated Parmesan, divided
Petals of 6 nasturtium flowers

1. Preheat oven to 350°F. Butter a casserole dish.
2. In a large pan over low heat, melt butter and sauté zucchini until tender, 5–7 minutes. Remove from heat and allow to cool.
3. In a large bowl, beat eggs with cream. Add bread crumbs, onion, Worcestershire sauce, hot sauce, salt, and 2 tablespoons Parmesan and mix well. Combine mixture with zucchini and nasturtium petals, stirring just until blended. Pour into the prepared casserole; sprinkle with remaining Parmesan. Bake uncovered 35–40 minutes, or until top is golden.

Brussels Sprouts ♥ Thyme

BRUSSELS SPROUTS is all about her exotic coiffure. She primps and crimps it all through the warm season, being careful not to let dandruff (in the form of aphids and moths) turn her 'do into a don't. THYME lends a helping hand by forming a carpet around his mate's feet and keeping her roots moist. He also deters the worms and butterflies that attack her sweet sprouts. Content in the same growing conditions, these seemingly mismatched mates are a match made in horticulture heaven.

Love Match

Both Brussels Sprouts and Thyme need full sun and sandy but well-drained soil, so amend with compost on planting. But from there they diverge. Brussels Sprouts is definitely the more finicky of the two. For her, timing is everything. It can take up to 4 months for her to sprout from seed, and she grows slowly (about 90 to 100 days till harvest), so calculate your planting based on when cold weather will hit. She shrinks from too much heat and will only produce when days are warm but nights are nippy. In fact, cold snaps cause her sprouts to sweeten.

Thyme is far less time-oriented. He happily spreads over the soil, forming a fragrant welcome mat for you to walk on. (Just watch out for the bees and butterflies that visit his pretty pink or purple blossoms.) He can be grown from seed, but dividing him into smaller plants is easier and quicker. Ask a friend to share!

My Place or Yours? Start Brussels Sprouts indoors 6 weeks before your area's last frost date. Place Brussels Sprouts and Thyme seedlings 15 inches apart in well-fertilized soil.

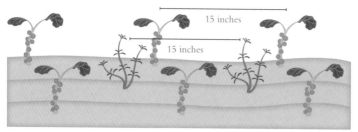

Plant Brussels sprouts in rows or a checkerboard pattern, with thyme filling the gaps in between.

Plant Profiles

Turn-Ons Brussels Sprouts loves to cuddle on chilly nights, happily growing right till a hard freeze. She matures from the bottom up, so harvest low on the stalk first. Remove the leaf below the sprout and gently twist it off for a sweet treat.

Turn-Offs Brussels Sprouts doesn't much care for Thyme's friend Beans. She also dislikes Strawberry, with her too-sweet disposition, and don't even get her started on flirty and tempting Tomato.

Needy Alert Brussels Sprouts has a large appetite, so amend the soil in her bed with well-rotted compost or manure. She also tends to be a little top-heavy, what with sporting that elaborate updo and all, so try to protect her from toppling breezes while still allowing a steady supply of sunshine.

Stalker Alert Thyme repels pesky cabbage moths, attracts beneficial insects and pollinators, and makes a great ground cover that keeps Brussels Sprouts' feet comfy. Diligent crop rotation will also foil evildoers and predators lurking in the soil.

Love Triangles Brussels Sprouts is very close to her Brassica family (aka the Cabbages) and has been friends with Potato, Onion, and Celery since their first day at seedling school. She's also good friends with Nasturtium, who provides a nice ground cover and attracts aphids away from the sprouts. This situation makes Thyme green with envy.

Roasted Brussels Sprouts with Thyme

Serves 4–6

A vitamin-C superhero, Brussels Sprouts is divine after roasting. Her nutty flavor is heightened by the addition of pignoli and thyme. Heaven on a plate!

2 lb Brussels sprouts
3 tbsp chopped fresh thyme
  leaves
¼ c pine nuts
1 tbsp minced garlic

½ tsp kosher salt
¼ tsp freshly ground black
  pepper
¼ c extra-virgin olive oil
½ c balsamic vinegar

1. Preheat oven to 425°F.
2. Cut bottoms off sprouts and trim damaged outer leaves. Soak sprouts in a bowl of cold water for a few minutes and drain well. Cut each sprout in half and arrange in a roasting pan. Add thyme, pine nuts, garlic, salt, and pepper. Pour olive oil and vinegar overtop and toss everything well to coat. Bake 20 minutes. Remove from oven, stir, and return to oven another 25 minutes, or until sprouts are nicely browned.

Kale

♥ Dandelion

The "bitter" rumor about KALE and DANDELION is what brought them together in the first place, and they've been sweet on each other ever since. Their relationship thrives despite adversity, thanks to their perseverance—it's tough to eradicate them from the garden. And why would you want to? With their tasty greenery and eye-catching colors, they add flash and dash to salads and stir-fries, not to mention an unexpected ornamental touch to the raised bed.

Love Match

Free-spirited Dandelion can't be tied down by the conformities of the garden and often rides the wind in search of greener pastures. You can easily grow him from seed but probably won't need to—he's known for popping up everywhere, and he's sure to come back year after year. His friendly flower is a composite type, the best for attracting bees and other pollinators. His blooms are as edible as his leaves, which taste best when newly emerged, before the flower stalks. Even his roots can be consumed in the form of wine.

Kale is in awe of Dandelion's ability to go where the wind takes him, while Dandelion admires Kale's head of ruffled leaves that look like fancy flowers. Indeed, this colorful and curly cooking green adds a fun and fanciful touch to the veggie bed. She's also quick to grow (less than two months to harvest), so the lazy gardener can wait till after the first planting rush to get her started. She loves cool temperatures and gets sweeter after a frost, like many in her Brassica family.

My Place or Yours? Sow Kale seeds directly in the garden, about ½ inch deep, 3 or 4 weeks before your area's last frost. Space about 1 foot apart, leaving room for Dandelion to visit. Thin Dandelion seedlings to 8 to 10 inches apart.

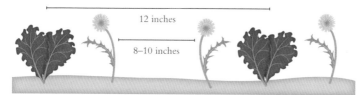

12 inches

8–10 inches

Sow dandelion seeds ½ inch deep, interspersed among kale.

Plant Profiles

Turn-Ons Kale likes full sun but shies away from extreme heat, so provide partial shade in warmer climates or time your planting for a cool-season harvest. Like many greens (à la Lettuce and her ilk), she likes to have her outer leaves picked. (Leave inner ones intact to avoid damaging her growth.)

Turn-Offs Kale is part of the Cabbage family and shares their rivalry with Beans and Strawberry. Dandelion has no grudges. He thinks it's bad for his taproot structure.

Needy Alert Kale copes with her mixed feelings about Dandelion's wanderings by consuming copious amounts of fertilizer. Spray her luscious hair with fish emulsion every month or dress her bed with compost, otherwise you'll never hear the end of it. She's also somewhat shallow (rooted, that is), so keep her mulched and moist.

Stalker Alert Nothing seems to bother good ole Dandelion, who is known for attracting lots of beneficials (notably, bees). Unfortunately, Kale, like many in her Brassica family, is hounded by a host of nasty bugs, from aphids and beetles to loopers and worms. Avoid planting her in the same place each year.

Love Triangles Kale and Dandelion have an open relationship. Kale is allowed to get chummy with Basil, Celery, Cucumber, Dill, Lettuce, Onion, Potato, and Marigold while the truly dandy Dandelion is off visiting other garden beds, lawns, sidewalks, cracks in asphalt, roadside ditches, abandoned lots . . .

Sautéed Greens
Serves 4–6

Kale is a bit too tough to eat raw, so this preparation method is perfect. Dandelion—high in vitamins A and C, potassium, and iron—is delicious raw or cooked.

3 tbsp olive oil
2 lbs kale, trimmed, washed, and torn into 1-inch pieces
1 lb dandelion greens, trimmed, washed, and torn into 1-inch pieces

⅓ c vinegar
3 tbsp sugar
Kosher salt and freshly ground black pepper

1. Heat olive oil in a large heavy pot over medium-high heat. Add greens and toss to coat. Mix together vinegar and sugar and add to greens, tossing to combine. Cover and simmer 10 to 15 minutes, or until tender. Season with salt and pepper to taste.

Garlic

♥ Everyone

GARLIC is a friend to nearly everyone in the garden. His charming guile and strong odor help deter pesky stalkers, which makes him especially popular among the ladies. Plus his green tops stand tall as a warning, just in case. Equipped with compact cloves all wrapped in papery leaves like a precious present, he doesn't require much room to grow. This popular easygoing fellow loves to mingle at garden parties, so don't hesitate to introduce him to all your soil mates.

Love Match

Garlic is a formidable fellow and surprisingly easy to grow. His one request: sandy but well-drained soil that's somewhat fertile (enrich with compost before planting). He prefers digging in his roots in chilly temperatures, so time your planting to allow him cool weather to grow and warm weather to ripen.

Garlic can be planted in early spring if you live in cold climates or in fall or winter in warmer ones. He's known for overwintering, which is a treat for gardeners looking to extend the growing season. He'll be ready for harvest after a couple months of warm weather. Wait until his tops die down to dig up the bulbs. You can tie small bundles together and dry in a cool place or cut off the tops and store them in mesh bags (like those used for onions). If you just can't wait, then roast and eat right away.

The "hardneck" types produce lovely flowers, called scapes. They're delicious when harvested early—cut them off the stem and sauté with olive oil and salt.

My Place or Yours? Plant Garlic cloves, pointy-end up, 1 to 3 inches deep and 4 inches apart in all directions.

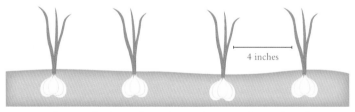

4 inches

You can place garlic throughout the garden, just allow a bit of room between plants.

Plant Profiles

Turn-Ons Although Garlic is proud of his green tops and wants to show off his pretty blossoms, sometimes he doesn't know what's best for him. It's better to cut off any flowering stems to redirect his energy to forming a clove-packed bulb.

Turn-Offs Garlic tries to avoid socializing with Beans, Peas, and Potatoes, who don't love his company. He gets the last laugh, though, when he joins them on the dinner table.

Needy Alert For good flavor and odor, provide rich soil. If your soil is not rich enough for Garlic, drench it with fish emulsion or compost when Garlic's tops peek out a few inches above ground.

Stalker Alert Garlic has adapted to many climates and is bothered by few pests. Maybe they're afraid of his strong scent, maybe they don't like his hard head—who knows. All gardeners know is that he has many virtues that make him well worth growing.

Love Triangles It's easier to name the veggies who don't like Garlic than all those who can't get enough of him. So spread him around to make everyone happier. He has an especially soft spot for Basil, Lettuce, Cabbage, and Tomato.

Garlic Aioli
Makes 1½ cups

Although repellent to some, garlic is a cook's best friend. Try this traditional spread with grilled or steamed vegetables, fish, or poultry.

6 garlic cloves, chopped
2 large eggs
2 tbsp freshly squeezed
   lemon juice

2 tbsp fresh parsley, chopped
Kosher salt and freshly ground
   black pepper
1 c olive oil

1. Combine garlic, eggs, lemon juice, parsley, salt, and pepper in a food processor or blender and puree. Add the oil in a slow stream and continue to process until the mixture has formed a thick emulsion.

Sweet Potato

Summer Savory

SWEET POTATO and SUMMER SAVORY are another unlikely pair who have defied the odds to become one of the favorite veggie couples, both at garden parties and on dinner tables. Summer Savory keeps his attention on the stalkers while Sweet Potato keeps her eyes on everything else. True warm-weather lovers, Summer Savory and his "Sweetie" love to bask in the sunshine and lounge in their raised bed.

Love Match

Sweet Potato can be started from a miniature plant called a "slip" (sprouts from a main tuber) or grown from seed, which is a fun way to raise this favorite native American crop.

She's a little finicky about her upbringing: She needs a long time to grow (up to five months) and stable warm-ish soil at least 55°F, so it's probably wise to plant her in a raised bed or one that's protected with a warm blanket of black plastic. Like her cousin Potato, she is planted deeply in a wide trench, with the soil mounded up around her as she grows. Be sure to always leave about a foot of foliage above ground. She becomes a sprawling vine that needs room to spread (though there are bush varieties if your space is limited).

Summer Savory also likes warm soil, so start him indoors a month or so before transplanting. With handsome blue, white, or pink flowers on nicely compact plants, this low-grower (about a foot tall) makes an excellent edging plant for your garden bed. You'll be sorry when he disappears after the first hard frost.

My Place or Yours? Plant Sweet Potato slips 18 inches apart in a hill or raised bed. Summer Savory seeds can be shallowly sown ¼ inch deep or scattered on top of prepared soil; thin seedlings to 10 inches apart.

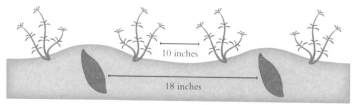

Plant summer savory around sweet potato slips.

Plant Profiles

Turn-Ons Sweet Potato starts working on her root structure as soon as she's planted, so provide adequate water and a dash of liquid fertilizer to help her along. After that, only moderate watering is needed, and preferably no drenchings, which will cause her to crack.

Turn-Offs Sweet Potato has dislikes similar to those of her cousin Potato, so don't invite Cucumber, Pumpkin, Zucchini, Sunflower, Turnip, or Tomato to the next garden party.

Needy Alert Sweet Potato doesn't like much fertilizer; it makes her sleepy. However, she does require phosphorus to be happy. You can provide this nutritious element by working bone meal into the soil before planting the baby spuds.

Stalker Alert Summer Savory cares for his mate by attracting helpful pollinating bees and scaring off sweet potato weevils, cabbage moths, and Mexican bean beetles.

Love Triangles Summer Savory is best friends with Beans and used to date Onion. Sweet Potato used to date Beans, so she figures they're even. Sweet Potato also likes to socialize with Dill, Basil, and Radish.

Sweet Potato Biscuits
with Summer Savory
Makes 15 biscuits

An excellent source of vitamin A, sweet potatoes are a tried-and-true old-time favorite. Pairing them with summer savory only adds to their delicious appeal.

1¼ c all-purpose flour
2 tbsp sugar
4 tsp baking powder
½ tsp kosher salt
¾ c mashed cooked sweet
  potatoes

6 sprigs summer savory leaves,
  minced
¼ c (½ stick) softened butter
2–4 tbsp milk (depending on
  the moisture of the potatoes)
2 tbsp melted butter

1. Preheat oven to 450°F. Grease a baking sheet.
2. Sift together flour, sugar, baking powder, and salt. In a separate large bowl, mix sweet potatoes, summer savory, and butter. Add flour mixture to potato mixture and mix to form a soft dough. Add milk, a little at a time, and continue to cut in until all the milk is used.
3. Turn dough onto a floured board and roll to ½ inch thick; cut with a biscuit cutter. Place biscuits on baking sheet, brush tops with melted butter, and bake about 15 minutes.

Garden Preparation, Planning & Care

Getting to Know You
A Primer on Plants

Let's start with a quick introduction to these unique and colorful beings: how they're described and categorized, what nurturing they require, and why protecting them from harm is so important. This information will come in handy as you start introducing your very own soil mates.

THE BASICS

As you've learned by reading the first part of this book, plants are as interesting and as individual as people. They have their likes and dislikes, strengths and weaknesses, habits and attitudes—in short, what makes them who they are. You can read dozens of books, old and new, about each one—and these will definitely help you find the right plant for the right place—but gardening is very much weather-dependent and location-specific. What works in a book may not work for you.

Here you'll find the basics about plants, but don't let this information stop you from trying new things. You'll learn much more the more you garden. A willingness to experiment will reap the greatest rewards.

IS IT FOR KEEPS OR JUST A FLING?

Sometimes at a garden party, a veggie thinks she's found the perfect partner, only to discover that her date is in town just for the season. Oh, no! Well, the same is true of gardeners, too. We fall in love with a plant and think it loves us back, but when the cold weather comes it disappears, never to return. If you want your beloved veggies and herbs to come back to your garden next year, you'll need to know whether it's necessary to replant them annually or if they'll come back on their own. Most veggies and herbs fall into the former category, but some can reappear without an invitation. Either way, rest assured: It's not you—it's them.

Usually, the heart-breaking desertion is due not to your bad hosting skills or lack of charisma but to simple science. Whether a plant is annual (dies back completely and needs to be replanted) or perennial (returns year after year) depends on its life cycle. An annual germinates, flowers, produces seeds, and dies in a single season. A perennial lives for more than two years; although it may die back when it turns cold, it will pop up again once the warm weather returns. You may also come across a biennial, or a plant that takes two years to complete its life cycle. But many of these—including carrots, parsley, and lettuce—are grown for their leaves or roots, so we treat them like annuals anyway. You can leave them alone if you want, and if the conditions are right they'll come back the next year to finish their proper life cycle.

In places that have cold seasons, most vegetables are grown as annuals. (Technically, a few, like tomatoes and peppers, are perennials in their original habitats.) That's because many of these plants hail from tropical places, so they cannot tolerate freezing temperatures. (Asparagus, strawberries, and rhubarb are pretty cold hardy and will be perennials in many gardens, even in the north.) If you live in an all-the-time-warm type of climate, then some plants—namely, tomatoes and peppers—may return without an invitation. If not, then you'll have to invite new plants to the party every year. You might be saved the trouble if the plant readily self-sows, meaning that it reseeds itself here and there. Of course, this habit could become annoying (fennel and dill are notorious for crashing parties all over the garden), but it's a nice way to spread the wealth of beneficial plants without much work. Also, if the plants that self-seeded are hybrids, you may not be able to actually eat them. So, what are hybrids? Well, they hate to be talked about behind their backs, but sometimes we have to gossip just a little.

A hybrid is the offspring of two plants that have been deliberately crossed to produce a better plant, whether one that's more disease resistant or hardier or tastier or prettier or whatever. Most vegetables that you buy as seedlings from commercial growers and nurseries, as well as many seeds bought in packets at the home center, are hybrids. These are fine to grow—in fact, they're great, because they've been bred to do especially well in your area—but just know that you can't save seeds from those plants (if you were planning to). The resulting plant will not be like the one you originally planted; it'll be like one of the parent plants (maybe) or some genetic throwback that might not even be edible. All hybrid seeds are labeled as such: Look for the word "hybrid" or the designation "F1." If you do want to try seed saving—and you should!—then seek out open-pollinated seedlings and products, usually offered by local farms and through well-established catalogs (see "Mail-Order Brides," page 108, for more information).

A FAMILY AFFAIR

Everyone knows that when the whole family gets together, crazy drama can ensue. Fortunately, in the plant world many veggie families socialize well with others at garden parties. Keep in mind that each family has its own set of cultural norms and habits (see chart, opposite), so be sure to plant members according to their compatibility with other soil mates.

BOTANY 101

Plants, like people, need a few essentials for a happy, productive life: sun, air, water, and food. Just like us, they take in these things and expel others. All the parts of a plant are important, from the tips of its roots to its terminal buds to its flowery tippity-tops. A plant is always working, taking in minerals and water from the soil, moving them up through its stem, delivering them to the leaves where its food is manufactured, and then carrying the energy back on down and around.

Family's Botanical Name	Members	Quirks and Eccentricities
Aster (Asteraceae or Compositae)	Lettuce, Endive, Sunflower	Prefers cooler weather and some shade in summer heat—except light-loving Sunflower, who always turns toward the sun. Pair nicely with onions.
Cabbage (Brassicaceae or Cruciferae)	Broccoli, Brussels Sprouts, Cabbage, Collards, Cauliflower, Kale, Turnip, Radish	Cool-weather lovers, hardy to frost and light freezes. Sensitive to heat; will flower quickly in hot weather and not produce heads (broccoli, cabbage). Like aromatic plants such as celery, dill, and onions. Dislike strawberries, tomatoes and pole beans.
Carrot (Apiaceae or Umbelliferae)	Celery, Carrot, Dill, Cilantro, Parsley, Fennel, Parsnip	Let the leafy members of this family go to seed, which will attract beneficial insects to help protect your garden.
Grain (Poaceae)	Corn (he's an only child)	Heavy feeder. Goes nicely with sunflowers, potatoes, peas, beans, cucumbers, squash. Avoid planting with celery, tomato.
Legume (Fabaceae)	Peas, Beans	Help feed the soil. Root veggies and beans like to be planted together, along with corn, coriander, and cucumbers.
Onion (Liliaceae)	Chives, Garlic, Shallots, Scallions, Leeks, Onion	Likes to hang with the Cabbage family. Interplant with lettuce, which will keep weeds from crowding onions. After harvesting lettuce, the onions will have space to create bulbs.
Spinach (Chenopodiaceae)	Beet, Swiss Chard, Spinach	Also cool-season crops; best to plant in spring and again later in summer to avoid the heat that can cause them to bolt.
Squash (Cucurbitaceae)	Gourd, Melon, Squash, Cucumber	To prevent fruits from rotting, place straw mulch underneath; anywhere they touch soil can encourage rot.
Tomato (Solanaceae)	Tomato, Pepper, Eggplant, Potato	Pretty demanding; like additional nutrients all season long. All members do well planted with basil.

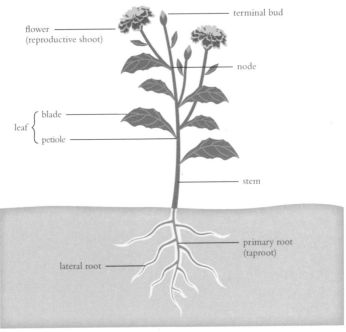

The basic parts of a plant, from head to toe. The stem can be thought of as the circulatory system, moving food and nutrients throughout the plant's "body."

Since it's primarily from the ground up that plants get their nourishment, good soil is vital to good horticultural health. The next section, "Laying the Groundwork," explains in greater detail how to figure out what type of soil you have and why you may need to do to improve it, but just know that you'll definitely have to get your hands dirty if you want to be a successful matchmaker.

The second most important factor in plant development is air. Good air circulation helps plants breathe, and it's also their best defense against a slew of pests and diseases. Plants love to sway in the breeze, so try to allow adequate air to flow around them. It can be tough to do once things really get growing, so plan ahead as best you can, placing or thinning plants according to the recommendations on seed packets or plant tags. And always be on the lookout for powdery mildew on your plants or interlopers feasting amid the cool covered conditions. The only thing you want chomping on them is you.

Of course, plants also need light and water to carry on their food-making endeavors. They absorb sunlight through their leaves and, with water and air, perform photosynthesis to make energy. Most vegetable plants need about 8 to 10 hours of sunlight a day, though some (like lettuces) prefer less time under the sun. Keeping them well hydrated is vital to their health and production, and many gardeners struggle with just how much H_2O is too much. For a few water-wise ground rules, see page 104.

Now let's discuss some specifics about the garden bed, since that's where love will bloom or disappointment will reign.

Laying the Groundwork
Bed-Making & TLC

Creating the ideal environment is the key to your matchmaking success. Learn how to make the bed properly, from the ground up, and your happy soil mates will reward you plentifully.

GETTING COMFORTABLE

When looking for any home, for plants as for people, the old maxim holds true: location, location, location. Considering carefully where to put your garden bed before digging in will ensure that all your toil and trouble will not be in vain.

Most warm-season veggies need a lot of light—about 6 to 8 hours of sunshine per day—so study your yard, balcony, rooftop, or wherever you plan to place your soil mates in order to learn where the sunny spots are. It's best to avoid trees, which will not only give your veggies the cold shoulder by keeping them under cover but also steal water and nutrients, thanks to the trees' overcompetitive root systems. Save the shade for your hammock and let your plants have their moment in the sun.

Before deciding where your garden bed should go, keep these things in mind:

* Most vegetables need full sun exposure, at least 6 hours a day.
* The garden bed should be close to a water source.
* Stay away from trees and shrubs with extensive root systems.
* Placing the garden near your kitchen will ensure easy access and encourage season-long care.

Once you've selected the perfect location for your love-seeking veggies, next you have to make sure they'll like their new home. **Rule #1:** Start with the soil.

Setting the Mood Before digging in, it's important to know a few facts about the earth underfoot. Knowing and understanding your soil is probably the most important part of gardening. Soil has to be *fertile*, first and foremost, but it must also have good *structure*. Fertility depends on the amount of nutrients it contains (and can hold), and structure is the layers and particles that make it up. You can improve both, but the first step is to find out what you're working with. To do so, you can test it yourself by buying an inexpensive kit (found in most garden centers or plant catalogs) or by contacting your local Cooperative Extension office to have them do it for you (for a fee).

What you want to know is how many nutrients the soil has, what type it is (sandy, clay, loam, etc.), and where its pH falls (whether it's acid, alkaline, or neutral). The pH is a vital factor in plant growth and is usually listed numerically on a scale of 1 to 14: Acidic soils have a pH below 7, neutral is 7, and alkaline is above 7. Most plants in general, and veggies in particular, like a loamy soil with a neutral-ish pH (between 6 and 7)—not too sandy so that it holds moisture, not too heavy so that it drains well, and crumbly so that the roots can grow freely and absorb maximum nourishment.

If your soil is not the ideal (and it probably won't be), you will need to amend it, adding nutrients and other matter that will eventually become humus, improving the soil's fertility and structure (making it more crumbly). The best way to do this is by mixing in organic matter in the form of compost. You can make compost yourself (see page 111), or your community might offer it for a small charge or even, if you're lucky, for free. Contact your local natural resources department, state park service, or Extension office for information.

MAKING THE BED
Raised beds are the best choice for most gardens—the ground warms up faster, the drainage is better, and the soil is looser. Raised beds may not

be ideal if you live in a warm climate, however, because they may get too warm or dry out too quickly. In those cases, planting on flat ground is recommended, and double digging may be necessary (see "Tilling Tips," opposite). The best time to begin making your beds is during the garden's off-season, in cold weather. By the time the warm weather arrives, the soil—and you—will be ready for planting.

Before diving in to your bed-building project, keep these points in mind:

* Dream big—but start small. Small beds will be less intimidating and easier to manage.
* Keep the width of the bed to about 3 or 4 feet so you don't have to step onto the soil for maintenance or harvesting.
* Allow for easy access by planning for paths between the beds.
* Aim for a north-south orientation so that the maximum direct sunlight reaches both sides.

Construction 101 Here's a simple how-to guide to bed-making. There are many plans in books and online, and everyone has a preference for size, shape, and technique, but the basics are pretty much the same.

First: Choose the type of material you'd like to outline your beds. The choices are varied, from lumber (real wood or recycled composites) to bricks to cement blocks to none at all. The one thing you should *not* use is any kind of chemically saturated wood, like old railroad ties or pressure-treated lumber—you don't want those toxins seeping into your soil and then into your plants and then into . . . *you.*

Next: Decide on the bed size and shape. A simple square or rectangle is easy to make and maintain—and therefore highly recommended. If you're using cut lumber from the home center, consider the lengths they usually come in. Anything longer than 10 feet is pretty unwieldy. Don't forget to include paths, and make them generous—about 2 feet wide. By season's end, those plants will be flopping and flailing and climbing all over the place!

Then: Mark out the perimeter of the bed using stakes and string or a simple hose as a guide. Dig a shallow (2-inch) trench inside the guideline so the first level of your chosen building material is sunken slightly into the ground. (If you think you'll have voracious visitors in the form of cute bunnies or gnarly groundhogs, you'll want to build more serious fencing. See "Rodent-Proofing," page 102.) Construct the beds using your chosen materials.

Now: It's time to till, meaning that you must dig up the soil and loosen it for planting. (See "Tilling Tips," below.) You can either dig out the whole bed, or just start removing the soil from the paths and piling it into what will be your beds. If you're worried about weeds or grass, line the beds with newspaper. Break up the soil as you go, removing rocks and other nonorganic debris and adding amendments as needed. Mound the beds 4 to 6 inches higher than the paths, filling the remaining space with good-quality topsoil or, better still, organic matter. Remember that the compost, manure, or other material added to the soil will provide essential nutrients for plant growth while also greatly improving drainage. Avoid walking in the beds to prevent soil compaction—you'll quickly undo all your hard work!

Almost done: Fill the paths with straw, wood mulch, gravel, or other material. You don't want to leave the ground bare, or weeds will quickly overtake them. Add a top-dressing of compost to the beds.

Finally: Start planting!

Tilling Tips To double dig or not; that is the question. What is the answer? Some say yes, others say no. Double digging means digging down and tilling at least 12 inches before planting. Is it necessary? Well, it certainly can't hurt, but it's probably belaboring the life of the average gardener.

For most vegetables, raised beds are usually sufficient for ensuring warm soil, good drainage, and adequate nutrients. If you want to plant really long, really straight carrots, digging deeper is recommended (though there are plenty of delicious stubby types of carrots). It may also be a good idea if you plan to garden on flat ground, but see what the soil looks like at 6 inches before committing to the full foot. It's a lot of work, but some gardeners swear by it.

Rodent-Proofing Wildlife is wonderful, but when they start eating all your food? Not so much. You may need to protect your beds from hungry animals who don't practice good gardening (or sharing) habits. Once they discover your sweetheart soil mates, there'll be nothing left for you. The best defense against burrowing bunnies, woodchucks, and the like is to use heavy wire (rabbit) fencing with very small openings (about one inch square) and to sink it *at least* a foot into the ground all around your beds. Aboveground it should be at least 3 feet tall, preferably with another foot or so folded over at a 90-degree angle. Woodchucks are surprisingly good climbers, and this extra obstacle should foil them. But they may still get in.

If you have deer, the only real protection is a really tall fence, about 8 to 10 feet high. These may be professionally installed, or you can try laying plastic-mesh fencing on the ground. Deer are notoriously skittish about where they put their hooves. But they may still get in too.

Bedcovers Most veggies like a nice blanket to keep them warm and hydrated. The blanket of choice is mulch, which will help retain heat and moisture, keep the weeds at bay, and prevent erosion. All tucked in under the covers, the frisky veggies can then concentrate on getting down to business. The best type of mulch is compost (see page 111 for tips on making your own), but other options include the following:

* **Shredded fall leaves** retain moisture and break down nicely, adding much-needed nutrients back into the soil. Just make sure they're shredded really well; whole leaves inhibit moisture from reaching plant roots, and they take forever to decompose.
* **Straw** is great for raised beds, especially in cooler northern gardens, because it retains heat so well. It's also friendly underfoot and is easy to till in after it's decomposed. Just make sure you get straw, *not* hay. Hay contains seeds, and soon your garden will be amber waves of grain.
* **Grass clippings** are usually readily available—just make sure they're dry and did not come from a chemically treated lawn. Grass clippings are especially nice for intensive plantings (plants close together) and those that love nitrogen-rich soil, like peppers.
* **Pine needles** are rewarding for veggies that like acidic soil, such as potatoes.

LET'S HOST A HOEDOWN!

You've done the party planning and now it's time to welcome your guests. Here are a few tips and tricks to keep the hoedown humming all season long.

The Way We Weed Once you've got the bed all shipshape, you'll find that a lot of unexpected guests will suddenly show up. Mulching will help keep the weedy crashers under control, but eventually you'll have to get down on your hands and knees and pull out persistent party-poopers. Try to nip things in the bud and nab weeds when they're young, before the roots are established. Pulling out bigger plants later can adversely affect the roots of plants you *do* want to grow. Pull gently but firmly, with your hand as close to the base of the plant as possible—you want to get all the roots (especially long taproots) or you're wasting your time. Weeding is easiest and most effective when the soil is moist but not too wet. Last tip: Try to do a little each day, say 10 or 15 minutes. It beats having to invest two hours all at once.

Refreshments Plants need food and water, that much we all know is true. How much depends on the plant, so take time to familiarize yourself with the appetites of each one. If you want a superabundant harvest, you'll proably need to be diligent all season long with putting out the snack trays: regular compost applications, foliar feedings, emulsion spritzes. (See "Aphrodisiacs," page 110, for more information on plant food.) If you're more of a lazy party-thrower, you may still manage a decent yield by side-dressing with compost once or twice, applying a dose of fertilizer midseason, and—perhaps most important—watering regularly. To avoid dehydration, follow these water-wise rules:

* Water long and deeply, about an inch per week during dry times (less when Mother Nature sends welcome showers). Shallow watering will cause plant roots to form along the soil surface, where they'll soon be burned by the warmth of the sun.

* Water in the morning, if possible. Watering during the heat of the day is nearly useless since moisture quickly evaporates, and watering at night leaves plants damp and invites slimy slow-moving gastropods to throw a slug-fest of their own.

* Avoid wetting foliage, which can cause myriad problems, including mildew and rot. Droplets on leaves may also act like little magnifying glasses that amplify the sun's rays, resulting in burns. Soaker hoses are great for ground-level irrigation in garden beds.

* Remember the beneficials. Setting water-filled saucers or shallow bowls right into the ground—like little lakes—will be a welcome oasis for thirsty toads and insects; stones set in birdbaths or ponds provide a handy landing pad from which flying friends like butterflies can take a sip and bashful birds can take a dip.

Special Guests Besides your lovelorn soil mates, who else should you welcome to your veggie-fest? Some people might not think it's a good idea to invite squiggly worms to a garden party, but if you're a gardener, they're exactly the guests you want. If your soil has lots of earthworms, that's a good sign, and of course they're the workforce of the compost pile too. Their castings (a nicer word for "poo") are an excellent source of nutrients, and their wiggly ways help aerate the earth: As they wend around underground they leave behind air pockets that help increase soil porosity and improve structure, making it better able to retain water and easier for plant roots to spread out.

Other bugs and insects help too, so be sure to be able to properly identify those you see slinking and flitting about before you decide whether to banish them from your bed. Read about some of the "Incredible Insects," on page 118, to learn more about courageous creepy-crawlies you'll definitely want to welcome over for extended visits.

CROP ROTATION

A change of scenery can do wonders for relationships. Veggies need variety to keep their roots strong and to rekindle the vigor they had as seedlings. To ensure that everyone stays happy and healthy, it's best to move plants every year to new spots in the bed (or to new beds altogether), a process known as crop rotation. Doing so helps maintain the soil's nutrient levels and prevents diseases and insect infestation from wiping out your whole garden bed.

When it comes time to rotate each new season, you can split the moving costs and shift everyone to the next bed together. The veggies can move back to their original bed eventually, but you should wait about four years to make sure all the stalkers have forgotten their address. Rotating crops is easy if you have four groupings of soil mates, like the illustration on the next page.

A 4-Year Crop Rotation Plan

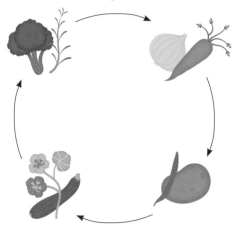

Changing neighborhoods is essential to good plant health.

NOTE TAKING

Many gardeners find it extremely useful to keep track of their horticultural adventures—bloom dates, exciting combinations, sad reversals of flowering fortune, and the like. A good old-fashioned journal works fine, but the digital world has made it neat and easy to record your gardening progress without all the mess and frustration of misplaced notes and undeveloped pictures. Starting your own blog (short for "Web log") is a fun way to save your memories for, well, ever. Blogs are a snap to set up; just visit one of the dedicated sites, such as Blogger, TypePad, WordPress, or the like. Upload some pictures, scan some plans, and start typing your way to a virtual garden journal. It's also a great way to connect with other gardeners in your community and around the world, sharing ideas and experiences and finding inspiration.

Foreplay
Seeds & Seedlings

Some veggies are ready to jump right into the great outdoors as little seeds. But many others lack the confidence to start their lives directly in the garden bed—they require coaxing and encouragement to make their first appearance. Usually, the cool-season crops are the most intrepid and can be sown directly in the ground. Warm-season plants tend to be shier and more delicate. Either they need to be started indoors from seeds, or you can take a shortcut and purchase them as seedlings from the nursery. The plants will require aftercare, mainly what's called **hardening off**, meaning that you put them outdoors for a little while each day so they can acclimate to the weather. Once they're toughened up, you can introduce them to their soil mates and settle them into bed.

Cool-Season Veggies

Asparagus	Carrots	Peas
Beets	Garlic	Potatoes
Broccoli	Kale	Radish
Cabbage	Onions	Turnip

Warm-Season Veggies

Asparagus	Cucumbers	Peppers
Basil	Eggplant	Squash
Beans	Herbs	Sweet Potatoes
Corn	Melons	Tomatoes

MAIL-ORDER BRIDES

Growing plants from seeds is rewarding, and ordering prized packets of tried-and-true heirlooms and new introductions from catalogs and Web sites is probably the gardener's #1 winter activity. Excellent sources abound, including Seeds of Change, Seed Savers Exchange, Thompson & Morgan, and Park Seed Company. But if seed-starting sounds like more work than you can handle, don't worry. Many of these same merchants offer seedlings too, shipped right to your door. And a visit to your local nursery or garden center will reveal a whole army of cute little baby veggie plants just dying (sometimes literally) for you to take them home.

SEED-STARTING 101

Many climates are too cold to start vegetables outside, and some plants require quite a long growing season. Pumpkins and watermelons, for example, need 3 to 4 months before producing edible fruit. For many gardeners, that's longer than their entire growing season! The charts on pages 122–125 provide helpful details about planting your potential partners, from soil temperatures to days to harvest.

Starting veggies indoors will ensure a longer, more productive growing season. The first thing to determine is your area's last frost date, which is available online, through your local Extension service, or from your gardening neighbors. Most seeds are started indoors about 4 to 6 weeks before that day. (Check the specifications for each vegetable to determine exactly how many weeks are required.)

Just as for bed-building, there are many recommendations for seed-starting, both online and in books. Here are the basics:

1. Use a seedling tray or recycled six-packs from the nursery, which are designed to maintain well-drained and aerated soil. You may be tempted to use yogurt cups, egg cartons, or similar containers—don't. Sanitize the tray and all tools before use by soaking in hydrogen

peroxide or a 10% bleach solution for 15 minutes.

2. Use soil-free mix. Seeds do better in it, and it's worth the investment. Loosen and slightly dampen the mix before filling each section about two-thirds. Allow the mix to settle—don't pack it in.

3. Sprinkle seeds on top. Sow at least 3 per container. Check the seed packet for specific instructions.

4. Cover seeds lightly with more potting mix and *gently* pat down. Some seeds require light to germinate and need to be covered only a little. Again, check the seed packet for specifics.

5. Sprinkle water over seeds. Avoid overwatering, which can cause seeds to mold.

6. Cover trays with plastic to maintain moisture and heat. Move tray to a warm draft-free location, preferably over a heating mat; the ideal temperature is 65°–75°F. Good air circulation is a must. Make sure to provide adequate indirect light. Many gardeners use "cool" fluorescent lighting hung from chains close to the trays, raising the light as the seedlings emerge and grow. (The lights should be only an inch or two from the leaves.) Check daily.

7. At the first signs of sprouting, remove the plastic covering. Make sure soil is moist, but not wet. As the seedlings start to grow, they need 12 to 18 hours of light each day.

8. Once the seedlings develop their second set of leaves, if they're sharing a single tray it's time to separate them and replant each one in its own container. This process is called *pricking out*.

9. When it's warm enough to transplant the seedlings outside, allow them to harden off first: Place them outdoors in a shady spot for a few days, then in sun for a few hours a day. Gradually increase the amount of time spent outdoors.

10. Once they can handle several hours outside, they're ready to be planted in your garden.

Aphrodisiacs
Organic Fertilizers & Composting Basics

Some veggies need a little pick-me-up during the growing season. The old "Not today, honey, I have a root-ache" excuse only works for so long. You need your soil mates to get growing! Fertilizing gives them a little loving incentive. Here's what you need to know.

FEEDING THE HUNGRY

In addition to water and air (and many micronutrients), plants primarily need three elements to survive: nitrogen (N), phosphorus (P), and potassium (K). What does each nutrient do?

Nitrogen promotes leafy green foliage.

Phosphorus encourages root and flowering growth.

Potassium aids overall plant health and vigor.

Compost is a great natural source of this plant food, so it's a good idea to add it to your soil when preparing the bed and then to top-dress the plants after planting. But at about the halfway point in the growing season—earlier if you live in a very warm climate or have a hot dry summer—you'll probably need to replenish the soil. You can use more compost or buy packaged organic fertilizer, which are available online and in select retail outlets (you may have to search a bit). The packaging will state the amounts of these three elements, known as the NPK ratio. Mike McGrath, who hosts a popular public-radio show about gardening and has been promoting organic practices for decades, recommends an NPK ratio of 3-1-2 for edibles, so look for those numbers or multiples of them (like 6-2-4 or 9-3-6).

Other types of solid fertilizers, such as bone meal, potash, or rock phosphate, are usually high in one type of nutrient and need to be combined to provide a balanced NPK ratio. Manure is tricky and may be too much of a good thing—its high nitrogen content may burn the plants. Use it cautiously or, as Mike recommends, add it instead to the compost pile, where it will speed the "cooking." Liquid fertilizers include fish emulsion and seaweed extract and are recommended for a small garden. They're a little more expensive, but their performance makes the investment worth it on a small scale.

THE DIRT ON COMPOSTING

Compost, one of the most reliable aphrodisiacs for the garden bed, is simply decomposing natural matter. It's a vital component of organic gardening and ensures that no harmful chemicals are seeping into the earth, your plants, or your body.

Compost can be made from garden, yard, and household waste or purchased from many municipalities at little or no cost. There are tons of different techniques and recommendations for building bins and where to put them, so investigate local sources to find what works best for your area. A shady spot is probably best, and it's useful to start on bare earth (that way, those industrious worms can work their way up easily).

The ingredients for this organic love potion are basically the same. You'll need a good mixture of high-nitrogen "green" materials (kitchen waste, grass clippings, weeds without seedheads) and high-carbon "brown" materials (shredded leaves, newspaper, wood). Build the pile in layers and avoid materials like grass clippings and leaves to clump together—sprinkle them out evenly. On the next page is a handy chart of what can and should not be composted. Remember: Everything you compost will eventually be used around your vegetable plants, so if you wouldn't toss it into your garden, don't toss it onto your compost pile.

Turning your compost regularly may give faster and better results, but all organic matter will break down eventually. If you don't think you'll remember or have time to turn the pile, just let it "cook" for 6 to 8 months. Place a tarp overtop to retain moisture and aid decomposition. Just make sure the pile isn't too dry or too wet. It should feel damp, but not soaking.

Dos and Don'ts of Composting

Yes	No
veggie and fruit waste (chopped up)	meat, fish scraps
coffee grounds and filters	bones
tea bags and leaves	fat
eggshells (crushed)	bread or pastry
newspaper, cardboard (shredded)	glossy paper, magazines
healthy plant material	diseased plant material
wood (small pieces are best)	dog or cat waste
sawdust (scattered to avoid clumping)	

So, how do you use your compost? You can either work it into the first few inches of soil (best done in spring) or add it as a top-dressing throughout the season or after all harvesting in the fall. Another method is to make compost tea, which can be sprayed or sprinkled onto plants, feeding them as they grow. It works wonders on the leaves, helping prevent foliar diseases and increasing the breakdown of toxins, and may even improve the flavor of the plants' fruits. To brew your aerobic tea, you'll need a large (5-gallon or more) container and an aeration pump, like those used for aquariums. If you don't use the pump, you'll end up with smelly anaerobic tea, which can harm your plants.

Alternative Meeting Spots
Gardening in Containers

Not all garden beds are king size—some are simply pillows on which veggies can rest their heads. Container gardening allows matchmakers who don't have the space, or the ground, to still enjoy the company of some of their favorite soil mates.

PILLOW PALS

Even the smallest patio or stoop can provide enough space to rest a flower pot, hanging basket, or planter box. Most veggies need at least a 5-gallon container per plant to flourish. You can still make room for soil mates to share a container, just get a bigger one. A metal garbage can will even work as long as you punch drainage holes in the bottom. Also, you will still need to keep certain containers of veggies away from others to avoid pillow fights and patio drama.

Many companies are now creating hybrid vegetables specifically to perform well in containers. Those that especially love the coziness of "pillow" living are:

Bush Beans ❤ Beets ❤ Broccoli ❤ Brussels Sprouts ❤ Cabbage ❤ Carrot ❤ Cucumber ❤ Eggplant ❤ Garlic ❤ Herbs ❤ Lettuce ❤ Onion ❤ Pepper ❤ Radish ❤ Spinach ❤ Squash ❤ Tomato (but stick with the bush types, labeled as "determinates")

Keep in mind that leafy veggies, such as lettuce and cabbage, can tolerate some shade, whereas root vegetables, like carrot and beets, need more sun. Tomato and cucumber, as well as other fruiting veggies, need the most amount of direct sunlight.

If all you have is a wee windowsill or two, you may want to stick with herbs and maybe some lettuce varieties or sprouts. Place the pots in the sunniest windows and turn regularly to allow even sunlight.

Salad-starting kits are also available and come equipped with artificial lights and everything.

KEEPING THEM HAPPY

Since you're creating a remote garden bed, you need to be especially conscious of the containers, soil, and feeding. A few things to keep in mind:

Choose the material wisely. Plastic containers deteriorate in sunlight, terra-cotta pots dry out quickly, and wooden boxes are susceptible to rot. Glazed pots with adequate drainage holes and redwood or cedar containers are your best bet.

Size does matter. Larger containers don't restrict the root size and allow more moisture to reach the roots.

Let it drain. Make sure the drainage holes are at least a half inch across. Placing containers on bricks to raise them slightly off the ground will aid drainage.

Searching for sunshine. The plants will need sun, so seek out a spot that gets at least 5 or 6 hours of light a day.

Soil specifics. What you plant your soil mates in is especially important because *you* have to provide nutrients that nature would otherwise supply. The soil must drain properly but also retain moisture to keep your veggies happy. Most gardeners opt for a soil-free mix, available at most home centers. Fill containers to about 2 or 3 inches below the rim to allow space for a little mulch.

Feeding time. Water and fertilizer can quickly be swept through containers, so devise a good regimen. Check for moisture daily: Poke a finger in the soil; if it's dry up to your knuckle, it's time to water. Apply a fertilizer according to the package recommendations, about once a month.

Beware of "bed" bugs. Even though your soil mates aren't snuggling in a bed, the same pesky bugs and disease can still wreak havoc on them. Keep a close watch and remove them by hand before they do their evil deeds.

Keeping Stalkers at Bay
Natural Pesticides

$\mathcal{P}$ lanting vegetables with their soil mates should greatly decrease the presence of unwanted insects and disease, but even the most compatible couples can attract stalkers. Natural pesticides will help deter them without turning your garden bed into a toxic tragedy.

Garlic Spray This mist kills aphids, mosquitoes, and onion flies and can fight off slugs too. Crush 1 garlic bulb and combine with 1 minced medium onion. To them, add 1 quart water and 1 tablespoon cayenne pepper. Allow to "stew" one hour and then add 1 tablespoon liquid dish soap. Pour mixture into a spray bottle, and your nontoxic spray is ready to use! Store in the refrigerator up to one week. (Just make sure your family doesn't mistake it for salad dressing, or they're in for a soapy surprise.)

Tomato Leaf Bug Repellent This spray can kill aphids, corn earworm, and diamondback moths. Simply add 4 or 5 pints water and 1 tablespoon cornstarch to 2 cups crushed tomato leaves. (**Warning:** Tomato leaves are toxic to your pets.) Strain the mixture, transfer it to a spray bottle, and refrigerate until ready to use. It works great on roses as well as veggies.

Salt Spray This solution is used for cabbage worms and spider mites. Just mix 2 tablespoons salt into 1 gallon water, bottle it up, and spray away!

Tobacco Spray This spray is great for combating many different types of bugs, especially caterpillars and aphids. Put 1 cup loose tobacco into 1 gallon water. Allow the mixture to set for approximately 24 hours; check the color. It should be the shade of weak tea. If it's too dark, dilute with more water. Transfer to a bottle and spray on affected areas. **Warning:** Don't use on pepper, tomato, eggplant, or any other member of the solanaceous family. Tobacco chemicals can kill these types of plants!

Soap Spray You can regularly spray your plants with soap solution, which will dehydrate most bugs and slugs, stopping them dead in their tracks. You can make fresh solution or use your old dishwater. Just collect some of the water in a watering can or a pitcher and pour it over the plants. This works well on hostas and mums but also can be used on other hardy plants. For a stronger solution, mix 3 tablespoons liquid detergent into a gallon of water; use weekly.

Baking-Soda Spray Combat powdery mildew, black spot, and other diseases with this handy spray made from a household staple. Combine 1½ tablespoons baking soda and 1 tablespoon oil in 1 cup warm water. Stir until the baking soda is dissolved. Then mix into 1½ gallons warm water and pour into a sprayer for immediate use.

Spearmint–Hot Pepper Horseradish Spray This hot blast works on many different kinds of bugs. **Warning:** Be careful chopping hot peppers—keep your hands away from your face (especially your eyes) and wash your hands thoroughly afterward.

   ½ cup hot peppers, chopped
   ½ cup fresh spearmint leaves, chopped
   ½ cup horseradish
   ½ cup green onion tops, chopped
   Water
   2 tablespoons liquid detergent

Mix peppers, spearmint leaves, horseradish, onion tops together with enough water to cover; strain. Then add another ½ gallon of water and detergent. To use, mix ½ gallon of the solution with ½ gallon of water. You can use this spray safely on almost any plant. Store this mixture for a few days in a cool environment.

TEMPTING TRAP CROPS

Trap crops are plants that sacrifice themselves for the greater good. They know going into the ground that they probably won't make it through the season, but they're willing to give their lives to attract stalkers, of the insect and animal variety, away from your main garden bed. The following crops have been shown to work especially well.

Easy Eggplant Colorado potato beetles love to destroy Potato and Tomato, but they love to nibble on Eggplant more. Plant Eggplant among Tomato and watch the insects feast on her luscious fruits. When the beetles accumulate, destroy the host plant.

Ravishing Radish Cabbage maggots, flea beetles, and cucumber beetles love gnawing on Radish. By planting Radish interspersed among your crops of Lettuce, Cabbage, Broccoli, Cucumber, Squash, and Pumpkin, she will attract all the pests toward her with her devilish smile. When the pests arrive, destroy the host plant.

Offensive Onion Onion and his family, which includes Chives and Garlic, will deter the carrot fly, Colorado potato beetle, rust flies, Japanese beetles, and aphids. The family's trademark perfume will also deter animals from munching on your garden, and you don't even have to destroy the plants afterward!

Neighborly Nasturtium All gardeners love to have this cheerful, bright-colored beauty in their neighborhood. Not only does Nasturtium provide welcoming shady hiding places for beneficial spiders and ground beetles, she will also sacrifice herself to aphid attacks (though these can easily be eradicated with a blast of water from the garden hose). Her altruism knows no bounds: She's known to attract flea beetles, slugs, and the caterpillars of cabbage moths, giving her life for her green friends.

INCREDIBLE INSECTS

Though bad bugs can destroy a beautiful garden in one fell swoop, some are amazing assets for pest control and pollination. Inviting good insects (known as "beneficials") to attack the bad ones is known as Integrated Pest Management, and it just makes good garden sense. You can search the Web for details about this ecological approach to reducing pesticide use in both large- and small-scale gardens. But for starters, here are a few beautiful bugs to live and let love.

Lovely Ladybugs and Lacewings These winged warriors dine on evil aphids. You can attract these fearless feasters by planting species they love, especially those with nectar and umbrella-shaped flowers, such as cosmos, dandelions, tansy, yarrow, wild carrot (Queen Anne's lace), fennel, and dill. The one thing they both hate is chemicals, so don't treat your plants with nasty toxic sprays or powders.

If the polka-dotted pals aren't visiting, you can try buying them commercially and releasing them into your garden. Do so at night (so *their* stalkers don't eat *them*), and only after a heavy rain or when the garden is otherwise moist (water it well if it's dry).

Bee-youtiful Bees and Butterflies Bees and butterflies are welcome additions to any landscape, patio, or rooftop. You should do everything you can to get them to visit since they will do nothing but good in the garden. They need nectar and pollen to be happy.

The matchmakers of the garden are **honeybees**, which help transfer pollen from plant to plant. They are responsible for pollinating about 100,000 plant species—wow! Honeybees are not native to the Western Hemisphere, but they are welcome nevertheless. Not to be outdone by their exotic counterparts are **native bumblebees**, which in the United States include ground-nesting bees, wood-boring bees, and bumblebees. Many types are completely harmless and are excellent pollinators. Don't shoo them—most don't sting unless provoked.

Perhaps the most welcome insects of spring and summer are **butterflies**. There's lots of information on planting "butterfly gardens" in books and online, including plant lists. Remember to provide food sources, shelter, and host plants and you'll be rewarded with colorful confetti in the form of flitting flutter-byes.

Here are a few tips for attracting these precious pollen- and nectar-seeking visitors into your garden:

1. Don't use any chemical pesticides of any kind! Ever! Seriously!
2. Plant large patches of flowers, especially fragrant ones (they love lavender! fruit-bearing trees too!), and mass them close together so the bees can see them from far away.
3. Choose flowering plants that bloom successively to provide continuous pollen and nectar resources all season long or year-round.
4. Go native! Opt for plants that are native to your area over exotic species. These include plants you might consider "weeds," like clover and dandelion. Contact your local nature society, plant club, or Extension office for a list of ones to try or keep.
5. Choose older heirloom varieties of plants over newer ones. Modern

hybrids are often bred to reduce pollen in favor of larger blooms, weird colors, or other characteristics the plant industry thinks gardeners want.

Spry Spiders These eight-legged wonders are beneficial to any garden ecosystem and should be welcomed with open arms—or at least not crushed underfoot! Some may hurt you if you're bitten, but those types are rare; the vast majority are completely harmless. Investigate the populations common to your area if you're concerned about poisonous species. Spiders eat loads of many types of bad bugs by trapping them in their wondrous webs. Just let them be, and they'll work their wonders for you.

Praying Mantids These impressive-looking insects are well camouflaged, so when you do spot them, it can be startling! Although they're some-what indiscriminate predators (they'll eat ladybugs and other beneficials along with all the bad bugs), they're still a welcome guest to your eco-logically balanced beds. Make way for the mantids!

♥

Metric Conversion Charts

Oven Temperature

F	C	Gas Mark
250–275	130–140	½–1
300	150	2
325	170	3
350	180	4
375	190	5
400	200	6
425	220	7
450	230	8
475	250	9

To convert other temperatures: From the temperature in Fahrenheit, subtract 32 and then divide by 1.8.

Volume

U.S.	Metric
1 tsp	5.0 ml
1 tbsp (3 tsp)	15 ml
1 fl oz (2 tbsp)	30 ml
½ cup (8 tbsp)	125 ml
1 pint (2 cups)	500 ml
1 quart (2 pints)	1 liter

Weight

U.S.	Metric
1 oz	30 g
8 oz (½ lb)	225 g
16 oz (1 lb)	450 g

Length

1 inch = 2.54 centimeters

Handy Planting Chart

Plant	Light	Culture	Optimum Soil Temp (in F) for Germination
Asparagus	☼	Transplants	65°–80°
Basil	☼	Transplants	70°–75°
Beans (bush)	☼	Direct sow	60°–85°
Beans (pole)	☼	Direct sow	65°–85°
Beet	☼	Direct sow	55°–70°
Borage	☼	Direct sow	70°–75°
Broccoli	◑	Transplants	55°–75°
Brussels Sprouts	☼	Transplants or direct sow	55°–75°
Cabbage	☼	Transplants or direct sow	55°–75°
Carrot	☼	Direct sow	60°–70°
Celery	◑	Transplants	55°–70°
Corn	☼	Direct sow	65°–80°
Cucumber	◑	Transplants or direct sow	65°–90°
Dandelion	☼	Direct sow	60°–85°
Dill	☼/◑	Direct sow	60°–70°
Eggplant	☼	Transplants	At least 75°
Garlic	☼	Direct sow	40°–80°
Kale	☼	Transplants or direct sow	55°–75°
Lettuce (leaf)	◑	Transplants or direct sow	40°–80°
Marigold	☼	Direct sow	75°–80°

Days to Germination/ Emergence	Spacing between Plants	Height	Average Days to Harvest
Up to 21	10"–15"	5'+	3 years, then annually in spring
5–14	12"–18"	18" to 4'	75–80
8–16	2"–4"	18"–24"	55–65
8–16	2"–3"	4'–8'	60–75
5–17	3"–4"	10"–12"	50–75
5–17	12"–24"	18"–24"	75–80
5–17	12"–24"	14"–20"	55–80
5–17	12"–24"	24"–30"	80–160
5–17	10"–18"	<24"	50–75
6–21	1"–3"	<12"	55–75
10–21	8"–12"	12"–15"	90–120+
7–10	8"–12"	4'–6+'	70–100
4–13	1–2 plants per hill	4'–6+'	55–65
7–21	6"–12"	<12"	Harvest leaves before flower stalk emerges
21–25	6"–18"	24"–36"	70–85
5–17	12"–18"	18"–30"	55–80
Overwinters	4"–8"	18"–60+" (greens)	Harvest when 4–5 green leaves remain
5–17	12"–24"	12"–18"	50–65
7–14	8"–14"	8"–12"	40–70
	7–14	10"–24"	50–65

Plant	Light	Culture	Optimum Soil Temp (in F) for Germination
Mint	☼	Transplants	60°–75°
Nasturtium	☼/☾	Direct sow	65°–70°
Onion	☼	Transplants (sets)	50°–85°
Parsley	☼	Transplants or direct sow	50°–75°
Peas	☼	Direct sow	40°–75°
Pepper	☼	Transplants or direct sow	70°–85°
Potato	☼	Transplants (seed potatoes)	Cool
Pumpkin	☼	Transplants	65°–85°
Radish	☼	Direct sow	45°–85°
Rosemary	☼	Transplants	60°–70°
Spinach	☼/☾	Direct sow	45°–75°
Summer Savory	☼	Transplants or direct sow	65°–70°
Summer Squash	☼	Transplants	65°–85°
Sunflower	☼	Direct sow	70°–85°
Sweet Potato	☼	Transplants (slips)	65°–85°
Thyme	☼	Transplants or direct sow	65°–70°
Tomato	☼	Transplants	60°–85°
Turnip	☼	Direct sow	60°–95°
Zucchini	☼	Transplants	65°–85°

Days to Germination/ Emergence	Spacing between Plants	Height	Average Days to Harvest
7–14	24+"	12"–24"	Harvest leaves anytime
7–14	4"–12"	10"–24"	Leaves and flowers are edible anytime
4–14	2"–8"	6"–8" (greens)	75–100+
12–28	8"–12"	12"–18"	70–85
6–14	1"–3"	20"–30"	55–75
8–24	12"–18"	24"–30"	55–80
--	12"	18"–24"	70–110+
5–10	3'–5+'	5'–10+' (vining)	95–110+
4–10	1"–3"	6"–10"	20–35
21–25	12"–36"	20+"	80–85
5–12	4"–8"		40–50
10–15	10"–18"	12"–18"	55–65
5–10	2'–5' (vining)	12"–24"	50–70
10–14	12"–18"	12"–72+"	Harvest seeds after drying seedhead completely
--	12"–18"	12"–15"	70–90+
21–28	12"–18"	2"–12"	70–85
6–14	24"–36"	24"–60+"	55–90
1–3	3"–6"	12"–14"	35–60
5–10	3'–5' (vining)	12"–24"	50–70

Index

Other Sources on Companion Planting

Sally Jean Cunningham, *Great Garden Companions* (Emmaus, Pa.: Rodale, 1998).

Louise Riotte, *Carrots Love Tomatoes* (North Adams, Mass.: Storey Publishing, 1998).

irreference \ir-'ef-(ə-)rən(t)s\ n (2009)

1 : irreverent reference
2 : real information that also entertains or amuses

HOW-TOS. QUIZZES. INSTRUCTIONS.
RECIPES. CRAFTS. JOKES.
TRIVIA. GAMES. TRICKS.
QUOTES. ADVICE. TIPS.

LEARN SOMETHING. OR NOT.

VISIT IRREFERENCE.COM
The New Quirk Books Web Site